Cambridge Elements ≡

Elements in the Philosophy of Science
edited by
Jacob Stegenga
University of Cambridge

VALUES IN SCIENCE

Kevin C. Elliott
Michigan State University

CAMBRIDGE
UNIVERSITY PRESS

University Printing House, Cambridge CB2 8BS, United Kingdom

One Liberty Plaza, 20th Floor, New York, NY 10006, USA

477 Williamstown Road, Port Melbourne, VIC 3207, Australia

314–321, 3rd Floor, Plot 3, Splendor Forum, Jasola District Centre,
New Delhi – 110025, India

103 Penang Road, #05–06/07, Visioncrest Commercial, Singapore 238467

Cambridge University Press is part of the University of Cambridge.

It furthers the University's mission by disseminating knowledge in the pursuit of
education, learning, and research at the highest international levels of excellence.

www.cambridge.org
Information on this title: www.cambridge.org/9781009055635
DOI: 10.1017/9781009052597

First published 2022

A catalogue record for this publication is available from the British Library.

ISBN 978-1-009-05563-5 Paperback
ISSN 2517-7273 (online)
ISSN 2517-7265 (print)

Values in Science

Elements in the Philosophy of Science

DOI: 10.1017/9781009052597
First published online: June 2022

Kevin C. Elliott
Michigan State University

Author for correspondence: Kevin C. Elliott, kce@msu.edu

Abstract: This Element introduces the philosophical literature on values in science by examining four questions: (1) How do values influence science? (2) Should we actively incorporate values in science? (3) How can we manage values in science responsibly? (4) What are some next steps for those who want to help promote responsible roles for values in science? It explores arguments for and against the 'value-free ideal' for science (i.e., the notion that values should be excluded from scientific reasoning) and concludes that it should be rejected. Nonetheless, this does not mean that value influences are always acceptable. The Element explores a range of strategies to distinguish between appropriate and inappropriate value influences. It concludes by proposing an approach to managing values in science that relies on justifying, prioritising, and implementing norms for scientific research practices and institutions.

Keywords: science and values, science communication, responsible research, research ethics, science and society

ISBNs: 9781009055635 (PB), 9781009052597 (OC)
ISSNs: 2517-7273 (online), 2517-7265 (print)

Contents

1 Introduction

The coronavirus pandemic that swept the globe in 2020 highlighted the myriad ways that values intersect with scientific research. For example, the speed with which the biomedical research community pivoted towards studying the virus and developing vaccines illustrates how important it is to be able to steer research so that it addresses what society values. Values were also obvious in policymakers' decisions about which public policies to enact in response to the pandemic. When deciding what kinds of lockdowns or mask mandates to impose, they not only had to assess the efficacy of various measures for suppressing the virus's spread but also had to weigh the overall social costs and benefits of taking those measures. At first glance, it might seem the policymakers could just 'follow the science', but it is clear upon reflection that responsible leaders had to consider a range of factors (e.g., economics, community well-being, individual rights, and mental health) when deciding how to craft their responses (Hilgartner et al. 2021). Leaders also had to take values into account when deciding how to describe the disease. For example, US President Donald Trump was criticised for referring to the 'Chinese virus' because of its tendency to promote racial stereotypes and stigmatisation (Viala-Gaudefroy and Lindaman 2020). Similarly, the World Health Organisation (WHO) faced decisions about how to describe variants of the disease, given the potential to stigmatise particular countries by naming variants after them. The WHO ultimately decided it was more responsible to name variants using Greek letters (Konings et al. 2021).

The process of developing, testing, and distributing therapies and vaccines was also awash in values. For example, the quick development of COVID-19 vaccines was partly the result of public–private partnerships, such as Operation Warp Speed in the United States, which helped fund vaccine development by private companies. However, because public funds played such a significant role in the development of these vaccines (and because the pandemic represented such a significant public-health emergency), some policymakers argued that the patents for these vaccines should be waived so that lower-income countries could more readily afford them (Iacobucci 2021).

Another important ethical debate related to vaccine development was whether to engage in human challenge trials of COVID-19 vaccines (Cornwall 2020). In this kind of trial, people are administered a vaccine or a placebo and then deliberately infected with the disease. This approach can speed the development of vaccines because the developers do not have to wait for people to be exposed to the disease by chance, but it also raises ethical concerns about the appropriateness of deliberately exposing people to a potentially deadly disease for which there are only limited treatments. Even in standard trials that did not involve deliberately exposing people to the disease, the designers had to make value-laden decisions about what populations to include. Initial trials did not include children because of a desire to protect them from harm, but eventually, companies began to design trials for children as well so the vaccines could be made available to them (Jenco 2020). Some researchers also worried that racial and ethnic minority groups were under-represented in trials of COVID-19 therapies (Chastain et al. 2020). Given that these groups were among those most severely affected by the pandemic, it was especially important that they be adequately represented in studies designed to test the safety and efficacy of treatments.

The disproportionate impacts of the pandemic on minoritised racial or ethnic groups also illustrate a plethora of broader ways in which the values of society affect the practices of science and determine how well those practices serve (or fail to serve) the interests of particular communities. For example, in countries like the United States, unequal access to economic resources and medical care contributed to a slower roll-out of COVID-19 vaccines in Black communities (Johnson et al. 2021). This was especially harmful because those same social disadvantages meant that Black people were more likely to experience pre-existing conditions that aggravated the effects of the disease (Valles 2020). Another factor depressing vaccination rates among minoritised communities was their distrust of the medical establishment, which was fuelled by past scandals and the legacies of racist science.[1] For example, in the infamous Tuskegee syphilis study that spanned four decades of the twentieth century, researchers observed the course of untreated syphilis in Black men without giving them information about available treatments (Reverby 2000). More broadly, the biological, medical, and social sciences amplified the racist and sexist values of society for centuries by trying to identify, measure, and explain differences between different races and sexes (Kendi 2016; Kourany 2010, 2020). In sum, the values of society have helped foster a context in which Black people in the United States are less likely to benefit from medical innovations, and the legacy of racist scientific and medical practices has some-times discouraged Black people from taking advantage of those innovations even when they are available.

This brief reflection on the COVID-19 pandemic illustrates that values pervade scientific practice, that the influences of values can be obvious in some cases and obscure in others, and that those influences can be both good

---

[1] See, e.g.,www.pewresearch.org/fact-tank/2020/06/04/black-americans-face-higher-covid-19-risks-are-more-hesitant-to-trust-medical-scientists-get-vaccinated/

and bad. Values can steer the direction of research, influence the design of studies, affect how results are described and interpreted, and guide the ways that scientific information is used. Sometimes, the influences of values reflect conscious goals or concerns, as when ethicists debated whether to pursue human challenge trials, but they can also be much more subtle, as when the racist history of biomedical science contributed to vaccine hesitancy. Values can be beneficial, as when concerns about equity prompted researchers to scrutinise whether minoritised groups were included in trials, and they can also be harmful, as when the language for describing the pandemic contributed to the stigmatising of racial groups or geographic locations.

This Element is designed to foster a greater understanding of this complex landscape and to provide recommendations for responsibly managing the roles that values play in science. Section 2 examines how values influence science. In the process, it clarifies what we mean by 'values' and the ways in which scientific judgements can be 'value-laden'. Section 3 explores whether it is appropriate to deliberately bring values into the practice of science and, if so, under what conditions. Section 4 considers a range of proposals for responsibly managing the roles that values play in science. Finally, Section 5 proposes a path forward for those who want to help promote responsible roles for values in science. Whether values are brought into science intentionally or unintentionally, they clearly have significant influences on scientific practice. Therefore, it is important to develop thoughtful strategies for harnessing those influences so that the power of science can be directed towards the greatest social good.

2 How Do Values Influence Science?

In order to analyse the roles that values play in science, this section begins by providing some clarity about what it means to talk about 'values' and their influences on 'judgements' in science. It then provides a systematic description of the many different ways that values intersect with judgements in science. This analysis demonstrates the pervasive entanglements between science and values and illustrates how important it is to think more carefully about how to manage them.

2.1 Values

In a very basic sense, a value can be defined as something that is desirable or worthy of pursuit (Elliott 2017, 11).[2] Once one attempts to elaborate on this

---

[2] This Element provides a broad definition of values, but it is worth keeping in mind that some scholars have argued for providing a narrower definition of values and a clarification of their relationships to the range of other contextual factors that can influence science (see, e.g., Biddle 2013). This is an important topic for further investigation.

definition, however, a number of difficult questions arise. Are these values desirable in an objective sense that is independent of what people actually happen to desire, or are they just subjectively desirable insofar as someone actually desires them (Brown 2018)? Building on this question, do values have 'cognitive status', in the sense that one can provide evidence for their desirability (Brown 2020)? And are these values actually qualities or states of affairs out 'in the world', or do they refer to the beliefs or concepts in our minds that represent these valuable things (Schwartz and Bilsky 1987)? Finally, what are the best ways of classifying these desirable qualities (see, e.g., Brown 2020; Schwartz and Bilsky 1987; Scriven 1974)? This question is important because those writing about values in science often lament that the word 'value' is used as a label for a very wide array of phenomena that ought to be treated in different ways (Biddle 2013; Brown 2020; Rooney 2017; Ward 2021).

For the purposes of this Element, I will set aside most of these theoretical questions. However, a crucial issue that pervades the literature on science and values is whether values can be distinguished into the categories of those that are 'epistemic' (i.e., indicative of truth or knowledge) and those that are 'non-epistemic'. Assuming that science is directed at the epistemic tasks of identifying true or reliable information about the world, one might think that only the 'epistemic' values that advance these tasks have a proper role to play in scientific reasoning. For example, building on the earlier work of Thomas Kuhn (1977), Ernan McMullin (1983) argued that the qualities of predictive accuracy, internal coherence, external consistency, unifying power, and fertility should be regarded as epistemic values because they are indicators that scientific theories are true. McMullin classified other values as non-epistemic because he did not think they promoted the epistemic goals of science. Importantly, though, he admitted that it is not always obvious whether particular qualities count as epistemic values or not; for example, he argued that scientists could learn over time whether a quality like simplicity actually serves as a reason for thinking that a theory is likely to be true (McMullin 1983).

It turns out that science is awash in values, and many of these values are not clearly epistemic. In addition to the values that serve as indicators of a theory's desirability, there are values that serve as goals for individual scientists, such as advancing in one's career, gaining recognition, generating discoveries, obtaining financial resources, and serving society. There are also ethical and social values that can apply to many different aspects of science; these include goals like economic development, public health, animal welfare, environmental conservation, and social justice. There are values that apply to scientific collaborations, such as being honest, giving appropriate credit, treating others with respect, providing open access to resources, and promoting equity and inclusion

(Rolin 2015). There are also values that apply to specific domains or kinds of science; for example, values like standardisation, reproducibility, usability, and efficiency are particularly relevant to policy-relevant fields of science.

Given the diversity and complexity of all these different kinds of values, the distinction between epistemic and non-epistemic values has proven to be highly controversial. McMullin (1983) himself acknowledged that a value could be epistemic in some contexts but not in others. Daniel Steel elaborated on this point by distinguishing 'intrinsic' epistemic values, which are constitutive of or necessary for truth, from 'extrinsic' epistemic values, which 'promote the attainment of truth without themselves being indicators or requirements of truth' (Steel 2010, 18). For example, Steel regards predictive accuracy and internal consistency as intrinsic epistemic values, whereas he characterises testability and simplicity as extrinsic epistemic values. Intrinsic epistemic values are always indicators of truth, but an extrinsic epistemic value like external consistency (i.e., consistency between a theory or hypothesis and a scientist's other beliefs) could be an indicator of truth in some contexts but not in other contexts (Steel 2010). Heather Douglas (2013) has further categorised epistemic values into those that count as minimal criteria as opposed to those that are ideal desiderata, as well as those that apply directly to theories as opposed to those that apply to the relationship between theories and evidence. Minimal criteria like internal consistency and empirical adequacy must be met in order for a theory to be epistemically acceptable; in fact, some philosophers argue that it would be better to refer to these qualities as epistemic criteria rather than values (Douglas 2009; Norton 2021). In contrast, Douglas argues that some desiderata that apply to theories (e.g., having a broad scope) are not themselves indicators of truth, but they can help evaluate the truth of theories. Because of the potential for values to be pragmatically helpful for arriving at truths but not indicative of truth themselves, Douglas prefers to talk about 'cognitive values' rather than 'epistemic values' (see, e.g., Douglas 2013).

All these distinctions might appear to be somewhat pedantic, but they are important because some philosophers try to manage values in science by allowing epistemic values to influence scientific reasoning while limiting the role of non-epistemic values (see, e.g., Lacey 2017; McMullin 1983). If one cannot maintain a compelling distinction between these two kinds of values, then this avenue for managing values breaks down. For example, Helen Longino (1996) has challenged the distinction between epistemic and non-epistemic values by arguing that the typical list of epistemic values developed by Kuhn and McMullin is not as uncontroversial or value-neutral as they thought; according to Longino, it is unrealistic to think that one can identify 'pure' epistemic values. Along similar lines, Phyllis Rooney (1992) challenged the distinction between epistemic and non-epistemic values by showing that non-epistemic factors can shape the ways epistemic values are applied and interpreted. More recently, she has argued that many values fall into a grey area that is neither purely epistemic nor non-epistemic (Rooney 2017). Given this complexity, the categorisation of values is clearly a topic that merits further scrutiny by philosophers of science.

2.2 Value Judgements

To analyse the role of values in science, it is also crucial to clarify the concept of 'value judgements'. This section provides an overview of what they are, what terms will be used to describe them in this Element, and what exactly it means to say that judgements are 'value-laden'. Speaking broadly, value judgements are decisions that involve the weighing of values, but these judgements can take multiple forms (Scriven 1974). One kind of value judgement involves assessing whether and to what extent a particular quality really is desirable in a particular context. For example, how desirable is it for a theory to be simple? And how important is it for scientific data to be made publicly available? Another kind of value judgement involves assessing the extent to which a particular value has been achieved. For example, to what extent does a particular method of housing experimental animals promote their welfare? To what extent does a particular theory exhibit explanatory power? Another kind of value judgement involves weighing the importance of different values against each other. For example, is it more important for a model to be highly predictively accurate or for it to have broad applicability? Or, when one is in doubt about the severity of an environmental threat, is it better to overestimate the threat (thereby prioritising environmental conservation) or to underestimate it (thereby prioritising short-term economic development)?

Kuhn (1977) famously argued that the assessment of scientific theories involved two kinds of value judgements. First, theory assessment requires determining the extent to which particular theories exemplify particular values, like fertility or scope. Second, theory assessment involves deciding how much weight to place on different values when rival theories display them to differing extents. Thus, Kuhn emphasised that scientific reasoning is not an algorithmic, rule-governed endeavour; instead, it involves complex choices (i.e., value judgements) on which reasonable scientists can disagree.

This Element will refer to 'judgements' or 'choices' rather than 'value judgements', but it will often refer to these judgements as being 'value-laden'. One reason for this terminological decision is that the language of 'value judgements' can be confusing for those who are not familiar with the philosophical literature on this topic. Those outside the philosophical community are likely to assume that 'value judgements' necessarily involve assessments of ethical or social values, whereas philosophers of science use the term more broadly to refer to any choices that involve weighing multiple desiderata in ways that are not rule-governed. Speaking of 'judgements' or 'choices' in general is less likely to cause this sort of confusion.

Referring to these judgements as 'value-laden' is a way to highlight the fact that these choices can incorporate values in subtle ways that are not immediately obvious. Zina Ward (2021) has provided a very helpful discussion of four ways in which judgements in science can be value-laden. First, values can provide *motivating reasons* for judgements, in the sense that scientists can either consciously or unconsciously decide to make judgements in particular ways because of values. Second, judgements can be value-laden in the sense that values provide *justifying reasons* in favour of making them in a particular way. Ward notes that it is important to distinguish between motivating and justifying reasons because someone could be psychologically motivated to make a decision because of one set of reasons even though there are different reasons that actually justify the decision. Third, values can serve as *causes* for a judgement even when they do not act as motivating or justifying reasons. For example, this could happen if values contribute to setting up institutions like universities or funding agencies in particular ways, and those institutional structures influence scientific judgements in indirect ways not envisioned or intended by those creating the institutions. Fourth, values can *be impacted or affected by* judgements in science, such as when the choice to use a particular study design tends to overestimate an environmental health threat, thereby prioritising public health over the short-term economic interests of those generating the threat.[3] This Element will use the term 'value-laden judgements' to describe all four of these scenarios in which values intersect with scientific choices.

2.3 Relationships between Values and Science

Building on the concepts discussed in Sections 2.1 and 2.2, it is clear that there are a wide array of judgements in science that can be value-laden. Figure 1

---

[3] Given the ambiguous way in which values can be thought of either as ideas in our minds or as things in the world, it is important to clarify that Ward is conceptualising values as things in the world when she says that judgements can impact or affect values. In other words, she is pointing out that judgements in science can promote some things in the world that are desirable (i.e., public health) over other things in the world that are desirable (i.e., short-term economic interests). However, it could also be fruitful to explore how these judgements alter ideas in our minds about desirable things (Korf 2022). I thank Drew Schroeder for highlighting this ambiguity for me.

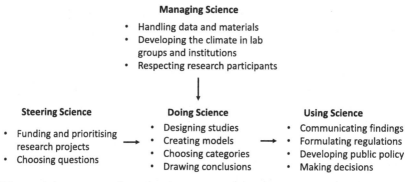

Figure 1 A representation of major ways in which values can relate to science

organises these judgements into four categories as a way of thinking about them in an organised fashion, but these categories are not intended to be mutually exclusive or exhaustive. Consider first the roles that values can play in steering research. The Introduction to this Element highlighted some of the ways that values steered research in response to the COVID-19 pandemic. For example, many scientists were motivated to shift their lines of research in an effort to help alleviate the suffering caused by the pandemic. For similar reasons (and also presumably because of economic motivations), policymakers and corporate leaders unleashed a flood of government spending, public–private partnerships, and private investment designed to support scientific research on COVID-19. Thus, the pandemic illustrates that values can steer research at both the individual and the institutional levels.

The ways that values steered research in the COVID-19 case appear to have been largely positive, but there are other cases in which values have steered research in very negative ways. For example, scientists throughout history have been motivated by sexist and racist values to search for biological traits that could explain the alleged inferiority of women or of marginalised racial groups (see, e.g., Kourany 2020). In addition, the desire to protect national security has stimulated research on horrific methods of biological and chemical warfare that are difficult to justify from an ethical perspective (Barras and Greub 2014). And negative value influences need not always be so obvious. There has been a great deal of discussion about the ways disciplinary boundaries can constrain scientists' research agendas in ways that hinder the solution of grand social challenges like alleviating poverty, mitigating climate change, preventing and treating disease, and addressing food insecurity (Frodeman et al. 2017; Kreber 2009; Weingart and Padberg 2014). One can frame this as a situation in which judgements about how research should be organised are influenced by values (in this case, the valuing of disciplines) that have been embedded in the structure of institutions like universities and funding agencies.

It is also worth emphasising that the judgements involved in steering research involve more than just decisions about what topics to study; they can also involve more subtle judgements about what questions to ask and how to investigate them. For example, Hugh Lacey (1999) has argued that scientists can study the same research domain using very different research strategies, meaning that they focus on different kinds of data and develop different sorts of theories. He illustrates this claim using the field of agriculture, where it is obvious that different strategies tend to support different values. Lacey points out that the dominant agricultural research strategy has focused heavily on questions about how to maximise crop yields by manipulating the genetics of seeds and by promoting fertilisers and pesticides. This is a powerful strategy that has increased crop yields significantly, but in some cases, it has had harmful effects on rural communities and the environment. Lacey points out that one could instead ask broader questions about how to design agricultural systems that alleviate rural poverty and that are environmentally sustainable. These questions could lead to alternative research strategies that would presumably incorporate greater input from the social sciences and from ecology. Lacey's analysis of research strategies and the values associated with them is applicable to many different fields. For example, the field of toxicology currently focuses heavily on identifying potential toxic effects of industrial chemicals. One could instead shift towards a focus on collaborations between toxicologists and 'green' chemists in an effort to design safer chemicals (DeVito 2016).

These questions about what research questions to ask can begin to blur into the second category of relationships shown in Figure 1: values associated with *doing* research.[4] This category involves the design of studies, the analysis of data, and the interpretation of results. Sometimes, philosophers of science have called this the 'heart' of science because it focuses on the process of drawing conclusions from evidence (see, e.g., Douglas 2009). This is the part of science

---

[4] Stephanie Harvard and Eric Winsberg (2021) provide an illuminating discussion about why the activities involved in steering science blur into the activities involved in doing science. They point out that scientific reasoning incorporates at least two activities: (1) representing phenomena and (2) drawing inferences. The activities involved in representing phenomena (e.g., creating models) straddle the line between steering science and doing science. On one hand, these representational activities involve choices about what phenomena to study and what questions to ask about them (i.e., steering science). On the other hand, these representational activities also have the potential to influence the conclusions that scientists ultimately draw (i.e., doing science; Elliott and McKaughan 2009; Okruhlik 1994; Winsberg 2018, 137). Harvard and Winsberg (2021) point out that the literature on values in science has been particularly focused on the judgements involved in drawing inferences, but it would benefit by placing more attention on the roles that value-laden judgements play in choosing and employing scientific representations.

where people have been most likely to think that values must be excluded. As discussed earlier, if science is supposed to be focused on obtaining accurate information about the world, then values – at least non-epistemic values – seem to be irrelevant to achieving that goal. Once one begins to consider the complexity of actual scientific research and the array of different ways that values can relate to this part of science, however, this view becomes more difficult to maintain.

Consider first the design of research studies. In an influential examination of previous studies on divorce, Elizabeth Anderson (2004) showed how researchers' values can influence how they conceptualise phenomena, which in turn influences how they design their studies. For example, she points out that earlier studies of divorce tended to conceptualise it as primarily negative, whereas more recent feminist research conceptualised it in a more open-ended way, as having the potential for both positive and negative consequences. Anderson showed that these different ways of conceptualising the phenomenon under investigation could affect how the researchers collected and analysed their data, thereby ultimately affecting their conclusions. To take another example, many environmental health scientists are now engaging in community-based participatory research (CBPR) projects. These projects typically involve collaborations between academic researchers and community members who have been affected by environmental pollution (see, e.g., Claudio 2000). Researchers who work on these community-based research projects often affirm that their involvement with community members affects how they design and interpret their studies, thereby ultimately making their work more responsive to the values and concerns of the affected community (Elliott 2017).

Another important aspect of doing research is the creation of models, such as the models used for predicting the impacts of climate change. Philosophers of science have identified a number of ways in which values can intersect with the creation of these models (e.g., Biddle and Winsberg 2010; Harvard and Winsberg 2021; Schienke et al. 2011). For example, Kristen Intemann (2015) has pointed out that climate modellers often have to make value-laden judgements about how to optimise their models; for instance, it might not be possible to optimise a model to predict both local changes in precipitation and global temperature changes, so scientists might have to choose between those two goals. Similarly, Wendy Parker and Greg Lusk (2019) have shown that when climate service organisations use models to make predictions about the future threats faced by local communities, they have to make numerous value-laden judgements about which models to use and how to combine information from different models. For example, if these choices are made in ways that generate worst-case scenarios for the effects of climate change, they serve different values than if they are made in ways that generate most-likely scenarios.

There are many other value-laden judgements that fall under this second category of doing research. For example, values can implicitly or explicitly influence the amount of evidence researchers demand before drawing conclusions (Douglas 2017; Elliott and Richards 2017a). Heather Douglas (2000) has famously explored this idea, arguing that scientists who study environmental pollution should consider the social consequences when deciding how much evidence to demand before concluding that particular forms of pollution are harmful or not. If they demand a great deal of evidence before declaring a chemical to be toxic, for example, they are relatively unlikely to make the error of declaring safe chemicals to be harmful, which protects the interests of those who use and produce the chemicals. Unfortunately, by demanding such high standards of evidence, they also increase their chance of declaring harmful chemicals to be safe, which harms the interests of the workers and consumers who could be harmed by them. Even in a theoretical field like physics, Kent Staley (2017) has shown that scientists make value-laden decisions when deciding how much evidence to demand before concluding that they have made a discovery, such as the identification of a new particle. Waiting to declare an apparent discovery could hinder the development of their research field, but announcing a discovery prematurely could embarrass the field and weaken its financial support from the public.

Philosophers have also shown that scientists make value-laden judgements when they develop and define the categories they use for analysing their results (see, e.g., Dupré 2007; Elliott 2009, 2020a; Plutynski 2018). For example, economists can make a problem like unemployment look more or less serious depending on whether they define the category in a more or less restrictive manner (Schroeder 2019). To take a different example, some Indigenous groups have argued that their communities have been harmed because researchers have defined concepts like food security, adaptation, and resilience in ways that do not accord with their cultural values (Bronen and Cochran 2021). Scientists can also cause harm just by using certain categories. For example, although the use of racial categories in medical research can have the beneficial effect of drawing attention to racial disparities in healthcare, it can also inadvertently contribute to racism by promoting misleading ideas about the biological significance of those racial categories (Cho 2006).

The value-laden judgements involved in choosing categories provide just one example of the many different kinds of value-laden decisions that can play into communicating scientific information (see, e.g., Elliott 2017; Franco 2017; John 2019). The judgements involved in scientific communication straddle the line between *doing* science and *using* science. Some of these judgements, like choosing categories, are closely associated with doing science insofar as they involve the analysis and interpretation of results. Many of the other judgements involved in scientific communication, such as deciding how to frame research findings when presenting them to decision-makers, fall more clearly into the category of deciding how to use results. A frame is a way of characterising or describing an issue or problem. For example, scholars have shown that one can frame climate change as a situation involving uncertainty or as an issue of unfair economic burdens or religious morality or public accountability. Some figures have argued that when scientists address a controversial topic like climate change, they should deliberately choose frames that are likely to increase public acceptance of their findings (Nisbet and Mooney 2007). Critics have objected that such efforts to influence public opinion could detract from the scientific community's credibility (see, e.g., Kavanagh 2007). This is just one among a wide variety of different kinds of judgements involved in communicating scientific information, which include decisions about when it is appropriate to advocate for specific policies (as opposed to merely presenting scientific findings), how much it is acceptable to simplify or interpret complicated results, and whether (and how) to communicate findings that could be misused or misinterpreted. It might be possible to minimise roles for values in some of these choices (e.g., by calling for scientists to simply present their findings rather than advocating for specific policies), but values are clearly important for handling other decisions (e.g., choosing whether to communicate findings that could cause harm).

Turning to other judgements involved in *using* science, it becomes relatively obvious upon reflection that values have important roles to play (Figure 1). For example, when formulating public policies, decision-makers have to draw on scientific information and then decide what goals are most important to them, what ethical considerations are relevant, and what costs and benefits to consider. For instance, policymakers and corporate executives have to take an enormous amount of scientific information into account when deciding what kinds of power plants to build. They need to consider the costs of building, maintaining, and eventually decommissioning the plants; the effects of the plants on climate change, local air pollution, and other aspects of the environment; the reliability of the energy they produce; and the likelihood of accidents or failures. This scientific information is not sufficient on its own for making decisions, however; decision-makers have to incorporate ethical and social values when deciding what kinds of risks they are willing to tolerate and what kinds of benefits they are most eager to pursue.

These kinds of value-laden judgements permeate policymaking. For example, when provided with scientific information about the safety and efficacy of drugs, the US Food and Drug Administration has to decide what kinds of risks and benefits to tolerate when approving drugs for public use (Stegenga 2017). Similarly, when legislators receive economic information about the effects of raising the minimum wage, they have to decide whether the benefits of wage increases for some people outweigh the potential harms for others. When local governments receive predictions about the ways climate change will impact their communities, they have to decide how much money they are willing to spend in order to adapt to those impacts. And, of course, when political leaders receive information from public health officials about the ways they can mitigate a pandemic, they have to consider individual rights, considerations of equity, and a wide array of social costs and benefits when deciding what restrictions to place on schools, places of worship, businesses, and private gatherings.

Finally, values also play roles in 'managing' how research is performed (Figure 1). In other words, value-laden judgements play an important role in deciding how scientists should treat one another and those around them as they perform their research. Ethical values are particularly relevant to many of these judgements, which have been discussed extensively in the literature on research ethics (see, e.g., Shamoo and Resnik 2015). For example, funding agencies and universities have to take ethical values into account when deciding what policies to implement for combatting sexual harassment (Mervis and Kaiser 2018). In addition, ethical values related to diversity, equity, and inclusion are important as scientists decide how to structure their departments and lab groups in order to create a climate that fosters positive experiences for groups that are currently under-represented in science (Cech et al. 2021; Settles et al. 2019). Questions about how to structure research teams and collaborative initiatives have become all the more significant as concerns have arisen about the dynamics of international research projects. Scientists are realising that the ways they share power, data, decision-making, and other resources in global collaborations can either perpetuate or help alleviate histories of 'colonial science', in which scientists in some countries or communities take unfair advantage of the resources and information available in others (Bronen and Cochran 2021; de Vos 2020; Pease 2021). Value judgements also pervade the ways researchers treat human research participants and experimental animals (Shamoo and Resnik 2015). Values involving fairness, allocation of credit, and career advancement suffuse decisions about how to allocate authorship on scientific papers (Settles et al. 2018). Similar values, as well as values involving the public good and the advancement of science, also inform decisions about when and how scientists should make their research data and materials available to others (Elliott and Resnik 2019; Soranno et al. 2015).

To conclude this discussion of the ways that values intersect with scientific research, it is helpful to make a few general observations. First, it is worth noting that values play a role in all fields of science, but those roles are even more prevalent in some fields of science than in others. Value-laden judgements are particularly pronounced in fields where scientists' conclusions have fairly direct implications for social decision-making (e.g., agricultural research, toxicology, environmental science, and many areas of the biomedical and social sciences). In contrast, ethical and social values have fewer obvious roles to play in deciding how to model, interpret, and categorise phenomena in more theoretical areas of science (e.g., chemistry and physics) that are fairly disconnected from social decision-making. Nevertheless, even in these fields, there are still extensive roles for 'epistemic' values like simplicity, explanatory power, and scope when deciding which theories are most compelling. Moreover, social values can sometimes play a role in these fields when deciding which projects are most important to pursue and how much evidence is needed for drawing conclusions (Staley 2017). And ethical values are obviously important for guiding the ways scientists treat each other in all fields of science. Of course, much more still needs to be said about when different kinds of values *ought* to play a role throughout all these fields of science as opposed to when they merely *do* play a role; the next section of this Element will explore that question in much more detail.

A second observation is that it would be misleading to draw overly sharp boundaries between the four categories of value-laden judgements discussed in this section. As Douglas (2018) has emphasised, it is not always obvious whether to place a particular kind of judgement in one category rather than another, and judgements associated with one category can end up 'bleeding into' other categories and influencing them. For example, as hinted earlier, it is not entirely clear whether to place the values involved in study design into the category of *steering* research or *doing* research. On one hand, one might argue that the judgements involved in designing a study fit well in the 'steering' category because they are closely related to decisions about which questions to ask about a particular domain of phenomena. On the other hand, it might seem more appropriate to place these judgements in the category of 'doing' research because they have so much influence on the ways results are analysed and interpreted. Ultimately, it does not matter a great deal whether one places study design in one category or the other because the value influences in these two categories do not remain isolated from each other anyway. Because the process of assessing hypotheses is heavily influenced by the body of data available to researchers at any given time, values that influence what sorts of data are collected (i.e., steering research) can ultimately have a profound influence on hypothesis assessment (i.e., doing research; see Elliott and McKaughan 2009; Holman and Bruner 2017; John 2015a; Okruhlik 1994; Winsberg 2018, 137). Similarly, because the process of assessing hypotheses is also influenced by the people doing the assessment and their background assumptions (Longino 1990), values that affect the diversity of the scientific community (i.e., managing research) can also influence hypothesis assessment (i.e., doing research).

Third, it is important to keep in mind that some categories of value influences are much more controversial than others. Almost nobody would question the idea that ethical values ought to inform judgements associated with the fourth category (i.e., managing research), including decisions about how scientists should treat each other and their research subjects. It is somewhat more controversial to decide what role different kinds of values should play in the first category (i.e., steering research). Some would say these decisions should be guided primarily by epistemic values, such as scientists' views about how to move research forward most effectively (e.g., Polanyi 1962), whereas others would say broader social values should play a more significant role. The third category (i.e., using research) is intriguing because both scientists and policy-makers often speak of 'following the science' or engaging in 'science-based' decision-making, which makes it sound like science alone can determine how people should make decisions. On closer inspection, however, it is fairly obvious that science alone cannot determine what one ought to do in any straightforward sense; one has to incorporate normative, value-laden premises about what one aims to achieve in order to make decisions that draw on scientific information. The second category (i.e., doing research) is the most controversial and has been the subject of intensive discussion in recent philosophy of science. Science is commonly assumed to be an objective, value-free endeavour (Douglas 2009), so it is natural to assume that non-epistemic values have no legitimate role to play in scientific reasoning. Nevertheless, this assumption has come under attack in recent years. Section 3 examines the debates about this issue.

3 Should We Actively Incorporate Values in Science?

As the discussion in the previous section makes clear, a more precise label for this section would be 'Should We Actively Incorporate *Non-Epistemic* Values in *Doing* Science?' It is fairly clear that *epistemic* values have legitimate roles to play in doing science, although there are still difficult questions to be asked about precisely which values count as genuinely epistemic. And we have seen that non-epistemic values have fairly obvious roles to play in the categories of steering, managing, and using scientific research. The really challenging question is a fairly specific one: should non-epistemic values play a role in scientific reasoning (i.e., the category of 'doing science' in Figure 1)? This section summarises the philosophical debates about this question. First, it clarifies some of the major reasons why many scholars have resisted allowing non-epistemic values to influence scientific reasoning. Second, it examines four major arguments for rejecting this 'value-free ideal' for science.[5] Finally, it attempts to synthesise the debates over these arguments into some overarching reflections on the current state of play in this area of philosophy.

It will be helpful to keep several caveats in mind throughout this section. First, as noted previously, this discussion focuses specifically on the roles that values play in *scientific reasoning* (i.e., the category of 'doing science', as shown in Figure 1); the influences of values on the other categories of activities shown in Figure 1 are less controversial, so they are not emphasised here.[6] Second, this discussion focuses on debates about 'non-epistemic' values rather than 'epistemic' values; it is widely accepted that at least some epistemic values (e.g., internal consistency and predictive accuracy) should guide scientific reasoning, whereas non-epistemic values have been the subject of the major debates discussed in this section. Third, this discussion is normative – it is about whether values *ought* to influence scientific reasoning. Almost everyone recognises that scientists are invariably influenced by values, and they typically cannot avoid making judgements that advance some values over others. The question at hand is whether the scientific community should deliberately take

---

[5] For the purposes of this Element, I am employing Heather Douglas's (2009, 2016) influential interpretation of the value-free ideal (VFI). On her view, the VFI asserts that non-epistemic values should not influence the 'internal' stages of scientific reasoning, which involve inferences from evidence to conclusions. As she interprets it, this means that the VFI is violated if there are sometimes compelling ethical or practical reasons for scientists to incorporate non-epistemic values in scientific reasoning. One could, in principle, interpret the VFI in slightly different ways. For example, according to Inmaculada de Melo-Martín and Kristen Intemann, the VFI requires only that scientists avoid making their own personal decisions about which values to incorporate into scientific reasoning; as long as scientists merely employ the values provided to them by other stakeholders, it would not violate the VFI (de Melo-Martín and Intemann 2016, 513). Moreover, de Melo-Martín and Intemann claim that their interpretation of the VFI is compatible with the notion that non-epistemic values must sometimes play a role in responding to scientific uncertainty; in their view, the VFI implies only that it is unfortunate when values have to do so and that, under ideal circumstances, non-epistemic values would not need to play a role in scientific reasoning (2016, 510).

[6] As Section 2 pointed out, however, the distinctions between the four categories discussed in Figure 1 are not sharp. Therefore, the arguments discussed in this section are sometimes relevant to activities associated with the other categories, such as communicating scientific information or formulating public policy.

non-epistemic values into account when addressing the value-laden judgements involved in scientific reasoning.

3.1 Reasons for Supporting the Value-Free Ideal

Let us begin by considering why it is controversial to bring values into scientific reasoning. If it is unproblematic for values to influence the other categories of judgements discussed in Section 2 (i.e., choosing research projects, making use of scientific results, and regulating the behaviour of scientists), why not allow values to affect scientific reasoning as well? There are at least three reasons for resisting this move. First, going back to the work of McMullin (1983), one might worry that values detract from the primary scientific goal of pursuing truths about the world.[7] If one adopts Steel's (2010) definition of non-epistemic values, they are neither constitutive of truth nor helpful for promoting the attainment of truth. If that is indeed the case, then these values seem irrelevant to accomplishing the fundamental scientific goal of pursuing the truth. Even worse, they could actually detract from the pursuit of truth by inclining scientists towards accepting hypotheses that promote non-epistemic values rather than the hypotheses that are most likely to be true (Hudson 2021). For example, scientists have recently worried that many recent efforts to replicate previous studies in fields like psychology or biomedicine are generating contradictory results (Harris 2017). One potential cause for this 'reproducibility crisis' is that scientists have been motivated by the value of short-term career advancement to cut corners in their research and publish work that has limited evidential support. Similarly, many commentators have worried that drug, chemical, and energy companies have defended questionable scientific claims not because those claims were true but because they supported the companies' financial bottom lines (Holman and Elliott 2018; Michaels 2008; Oreskes and Conway 2010).

A second reason for keeping values out of scientific reasoning is that it protects the autonomy of decision-makers (Betz 2013). One could apply this reasoning both at an individual level (e.g., we want to allow people to make decisions that accord with their own values) and at a political level (e.g., we want to ensure that democratic institutions do not inappropriately privilege some priorities or value orientations at the expense of others). If one were to allow scientists to incorporate values in their work, so the argument goes, decision-makers who made use of that work might not be able to make decisions that accorded with their own values. Wendy Parker and Greg Lusk (2019) have

---

[7] This argument presumes, of course, that the primary goal of science is to pursue truths about the world; one could challenge this assumption.

illustrated this worry by describing a scenario in which a local municipality needs to make decisions about its future water supply. One can imagine that the municipality might contract with a 'climate services' organisation to predict future water availability. However, there are likely to be a wide range of value-laden judgements that go into a prediction of this sort. If the scientists at the climate services organisation made these judgements in ways that did not match the values of the municipal leaders (e.g., if the municipal leaders were concerned about worst-case scenarios whereas the scientists were not), this could seriously hamper their decision-making. With these kinds of scenarios in mind, one might recommend that scientists should avoid making value-laden judgements so they can ensure that their claims are useful for all decision-makers, regardless of their values.[8]

It is noteworthy that this argument against incorporating values in science could potentially be used not only to challenge the use of non-epistemic values but also to challenge appeals to epistemic values when there are significant disagreements about how to interpret or prioritise them. For example, consider a scenario in which a group of researchers appealed to a particular set of epistemic values, such as simplicity and scope, in support of their decision to accept a theory. Assuming that the researchers had to make decisions about the extent to which those values were realised and the ways they should be weighed relative to other values, other scientists or decision-makers might not agree with those decisions. Thus, one could argue that researchers should not appeal to such values but should instead draw conclusions only based on straightforward epistemic criteria that everyone can agree on, like internal consistency and predictive accuracy.[9]

A third reason for keeping values out of scientific reasoning is to preserve public trust in science. It is much easier to engage in effective public policy-making when people trust the scientific information that informs the policy process. Liam Kofi Bright (2018) points out that this is one of the main arguments that W. E. B. du Bois gave for maintaining value-free science. Du Bois argued that in order to use science to improve society, it is crucial that science be trusted. However, he thought that people will not trust science if they

---

[8] One might argue that it is totally unrealistic to think that scientists could avoid making value-laden judgements, especially when developing models or choosing conceptual categories and terminology. For models or categories to be useful, so the argument goes, they will undoubtedly meet the interests of some decision-makers better than others. These sorts of arguments about the feasibility of avoiding value-laden judgements will be considered later in Section 3.

[9] Of course, a potential objection to this line of argument is that there could turn out to be disagreements about how to apply and interpret even seemingly straightforward epistemic criteria. Thus, it might be unrealistic to think that scientists could ever avoid privileging certain forms of reasoning with which others might disagree. I thank Kristen Intemann for highlighting this point for me.

think scientists are motivated by goals other than the pursuit of truth. Thus, he concluded that scientists should avoid incorporating non-epistemic values in their reasoning in order that the ultimate goal of using science to improve society can be realised (Bright 2018). Of course, this argument relies on the assumption that people will in fact trust science less if scientists incorporate values in their reasoning. The empirical evidence regarding this point is complex (Elliott et al. 2017), but it does seem plausible that science's authority in society is strengthened when people think science is focused on the truth rather than on other values that appear to detract from the search for truth (Holman and Wilholt 2022). Moreover, in addition to this descriptive argument, one could make the normative argument that people *should* in fact trust scientific claims more if they know that scientists are not surreptitiously smuggling their own potentially idiosyncratic values into their reasoning (Boulicault and Schroeder 2021; Schroeder 2021a).

3.2 The Gap Argument

Despite the appeal of the notion that scientific reasoning should remain value-free, philosophers have recently provided a number of arguments challenging this idea (see, e.g., Douglas 2016; Kincaid et al. 2007; Machamer and Wolters 2004). Four of the most influential lines of critique are what I will call the gap, error, aims, and conceptual arguments.[10] Helen Longino (1990) has been a particularly influential proponent of the gap argument (see also Howard 2009; Nelson 1990). (Table 1 provides an overview of this argument and the ensuing debates that have developed in response to it.) Building on feminists' observations that many fields of science had been subtly influenced by masculine biases (see, e.g., Keller and Longino 1996), she argued that there is an unavoidable logical gap between scientific data and the hypotheses they are meant to support (Longino 1990). In other words, she insisted that background assumptions are always necessary to establish which data actually count as evidence for which hypotheses, and she noted that those assumptions are often guided or influenced by values of various sorts. For example, during the middle of the twentieth century, many archaeologists argued that men's hunting activities played a crucial role in human evolution because those activities contributed to the development of greater cognitive abilities, cooperative behaviours, and tool use. However, feminist archaeologists in the 1970s pointed out that those

---

[10] There is room for debate about the extent to which these four arguments are actually conceptually distinct. For example, Christopher ChoGlueck (2018) has argued that the error argument is actually a special case of the gap argument, and Matt Brown (2020) combines several of these arguments under the general framework of a 'contingency' argument for values in science. I have distinguished these four arguments for heuristic purposes, but I acknowledge that the relationships between them merit further discussion.

Table 1 A brief overview of the gap argument, together with a major objection
and responses to it

Argument	Objection	Responses
Evidential gaps between data and conclusions are inevitably filled by value-laden background assumptions, and thus, it does not make sense to exclude non-epistemic values from scientific reasoning (see, e.g., Longino 1990).	Even if non-epistemic values *do* influence background assumptions, it does not automatically make their influences *legitimate* (Intemann 2005); thus, one could try to assess background assumptions based solely on epistemic values.	Sometimes conclusions need to be drawn before evidence and epistemic values alone can settle the matter (Biddle 2013). There may not be a compelling distinction between epistemic and non-epistemic values (Longino 1996).

advances in human evolution could just as well have been driven by women's gathering activities. Therefore, deciding which theory of human evolution to accept (i.e., 'Man the Hunter' or 'Woman the Gatherer') could not be settled solely by looking at the available data about the human advances that took place; it also depended on background assumptions about which activities were responsible for those advances (Elliott 2017, 70; Zihlman 1985).[11]

This 'gap' argument can be developed in a variety of different ways (Biddle 2013; Brown 2020; Intemann 2005), but the fundamental idea is that the available evidence does not determine which hypotheses or theories are correct in the absence of additional background assumptions. In addition, Longino argues that non-epistemic values cannot be excluded from influencing these background assumptions. For example, the background assumptions that supported traditional archaeological theories about the significance of men's hunting activities for human evolution were plausibly influenced by 'androcentric' (i.e., male-centred) values. Therefore, Longino argues that the best strategy for maintaining the objectivity and trustworthiness of science is not to try to eliminate values from science but rather to create a social context in which background assumptions and the values associated with them are subjected to critical scrutiny (Longino 1990, 2002).

---

[11] The feminist critique can also go further and question the assumption that it was men doing the hunting and women doing the gathering.

This argument has not escaped criticism, however. Kristen Intemann (2005) has pointed out that it is not enough for critics of the value-free ideal to highlight the existence of an evidential gap that *can* be filled by non-epistemic values; instead, they need to show that non-epistemic values have a *legitimate* role to play in filling these gaps. After all, even the proponents of the value-free ideal acknowledge that it is almost impossible to prevent non-epistemic values from influencing scientists' reasoning; they just regard these non-epistemic influences as biasing factors that should be eliminated to the greatest extent feasible. Thus, the proponents of the value-free ideal would insist that researchers should strive to evaluate the quality of their background assumptions based solely on evidence and epistemic values and eliminate the influences of non-epistemic values whenever they recognise them.

Nevertheless, there are a number of ways that one can defend the gap argument in response to this criticism. One option is to point out that at least in the short term, evidence and epistemic values are typically inadequate to determine which background assumptions are most compelling. Thus, scientists generally find themselves in a situation of 'transient underdetermination', meaning that for the time being, evidential considerations are not sufficient to determine what theory or hypothesis they should accept (Biddle 2013). The crucial point made by those who accept the gap argument is that it is often impractical for scientists to withhold their judgement in the face of this transient underdetermination. Even though scientists might ultimately collect enough evidence to be able to choose background assumptions based solely on epistemic grounds, for the time being, they might have no choice other than to rely on non-epistemic values (Biddle 2013). In addition, even when researchers do not intentionally appeal to non-epistemic values when choosing background assumptions in these situations of transient underdetermination, their choices still frequently have non-epistemic consequences. (In Zina Ward's (2021) terminology, values may play a role in these decisions as 'effects' of the scientists' judgements even if the values do not act as 'reasons' for those judgements.) Thus, it is arguably better for scientists to consider these non-epistemic consequences in an intentional fashion rather than making these underdetermined choices without concern for their impacts on society (Elliott 2017).

One can also defend the gap argument without appealing to transient underdetermination. For example, one could argue that it is impossible to draw clear distinctions between epistemic and non-epistemic values when assessing background assumptions (Longino 1996; Rooney 1992). According to this view, if values of some sort play an unavoidable role in choosing background assumptions, it makes no sense to try to exclude non-epistemic values from this process. Thus, debates about the distinction between epistemic and non-epistemic values play a significant role in assessing the cogency of the gap argument in situations where scientists have extended periods of time to evaluate hypotheses. Over the short term, however, scientists almost invariably face situations of transient underdetermination, so it is often unrealistic to expect them to abide by the value-free ideal.

3.3 The Error Argument

The second, 'error' argument against the value-free ideal is grounded in the realisation that scientists always face the risk of error when they make inductive inferences; in other words, they face 'inductive risk'.[12] (See Table 2 for an overview of this section's discussion of the error argument.) As a result of this risk, they have to make value-laden decisions about how much evidence to demand before they draw conclusions. Building on earlier work by Richard Rudner (1953), Heather Douglas has formulated the error argument in a particularly compelling way (see, e.g., Douglas 2000, 2009, 2017, 2021). She emphasises that scientists face uncertainty not only at the point when they draw a conclusion from the available evidence but also at a number of other stages throughout the process of enquiry, including the choice of methodology, the characterisation of data, and the interpretation of results (Douglas 2000). Moreover, choices at all these stages can affect whether researchers are ultimately more likely to err on the side of a false-positive or a false-negative conclusion. In addition, Douglas argues that scientists, like all moral agents, have responsibilities to avoid recklessly or negligently causing harm to others (Douglas 2009). Because of these responsibilities, she concludes that scientists ought to take the downstream social consequences of their potential errors into account when deciding how to handle all the inductively risky choices that permeate their work. In other words, she argues that scientists need to incorporate non-epistemic values in their reasoning.

To illustrate this argument in more detail, let us consider the example that Douglas (2000) herself explores in detail. She examines toxicology studies of the chemical dioxin, which is a potent human carcinogen.[13] Toxicologists who study chemicals like dioxin typically expose rats or other animals to

---

[12] As discussed later, the error argument could be expanded to include the risks of other kinds of epistemic errors in addition to those associated with making inductive inferences (see, e.g., Biddle and Kukla 2017; Harvard and Winsberg 2021).

[13] Technically, dioxin consists of a family of related chemicals.

Table 2 A brief overview of the error argument, together with major objections and responses

Argument	Objections	Responses
When scientists face epistemic risks, they ought to factor the non-epistemic values at stake into their decisions about how to navigate the risks. For example, because of inductive risk, scientists ought to incorporate non-epistemic values into decisions about how much evidence to demand in order to accept or reject hypotheses (e.g., Douglas 2009).	Scientists can avoid inductive risk by reporting probabilities rather than accepting or rejecting hypotheses (Jeffrey 1956).	There are still inductive risks associated with reporting probabilities (e.g., Steel 2012).
	Scientists can focus solely on epistemic values when navigating inductive risk.	To focus solely on epistemic values is unrealistic and unethical (Douglas 2017).
	Scientists can avoid inductive risk by hedging their claims and deferring value-laden decisions to others (e.g., Betz 2013).	Hedging and deferral are not always realistic or conducive to good decision-making (e.g., Havstad and Brown 2017).
	Individual scientists should maintain fixed, high standards of evidence, so they need not directly consider non-epistemic values when responding to inductive risk (John 2015b).	There can be significant social costs to maintaining fixed, high standards of evidence, and the benefits are not as clear as they might seem.

varying doses of the chemical under investigation. When they study slides of tissues taken from the experimental animals, they often have to make judgements about whether ambiguous slides provide evidence for malignant tumours or not. Then, when they analyse the resulting data, they have to decide what level of statistical significance to demand in order to conclude that the chemical under investigation increased cancer rates in the experimental animals. Finally, they have to extrapolate from the results obtained at high doses in experimental animals to the results they would be likely to observe at lower doses in humans. At all these stages and many others throughout the course of enquiry, the toxicologists have to make choices. If they make these choices in some ways, they are more likely to conclude that the chemical under investigation is harmful, even though it might not be. If they make the choices in other ways, they are more likely to conclude that the chemical is not harmful, even though it might be. Douglas argues that the scientists doing this research ought to consider a range of ethical considerations – for example, the costs to the chemical industry of falsely considering the chemical to be harmful and the costs to public health from falsely considering the chemical to be safe – when deciding how to handle these choices.

Justin Biddle and Quill Kukla (writing as Rebecca Kukla; 2017) have argued that the inductive risks studied by Douglas are just one category of a broad landscape of different kinds of epistemic risks that could be considered under the scope of the error argument. They define epistemic risk as 'any risk of epistemic error that arises anywhere during knowledge practices' (Biddle and Kukla 2017, 218). In addition to inductive risk, which they define as 'the risk of wrongly accepting or rejecting a hypothesis on the basis of evidence' (Biddle and Kukla 2017, 218), they point out that scientists face epistemic risks when deciding how to operationalise their concepts, when deciding whether to exclude or include borderline data points, and when deciding which models to employ.

One might argue that the other epistemic risks discussed by Biddle and Kukla can be subsumed under the umbrella of inductive risk insofar as they ultimately have the downstream effect of contributing to wrongly accepting or rejecting hypotheses (Douglas 2000). For example, the decision to exclude a data point might make scientists more likely to make the false-negative error of rejecting a hypothesis that is actually true. However, Stephanie Harvard and Eric Winsberg (2021) contend that some epistemic risks can have additional effects in addition to any downstream effects they might have on hypothesis acceptance. They introduce the concept of 'representational risk', which consists in making a representational decision that is inadequate to the purpose of the representation. For example, a representational decision could end up obscuring desired information or providing answers to irrelevant, misleading, or harmful questions. For instance, those who design clinical trials sometimes have several different conditions that they could use as a 'control' for the purposes of studying the efficacy and safety of a new drug treatment, and the choice of a control condition that helps medical professionals answer one set of questions might be unhelpful and even misleading for answering other questions about the drug under investigation. Harvard and Winsberg (2021) argue that representational risks need not always generate inductive risks (which they define as the risk of inferring a false fact), and they can generate other downstream risks in addition to inductive risks. For the purposes of this Element, we can focus on the concept of inductive risk while recognising that the error argument could be extended to include other epistemic risks.[14]

Some of the major objections to the error argument were already developed in response to Rudner's initial formulation of it in the mid-twentieth century. Richard Jeffrey (1956) argued that scientists could escape the force of the argument if they avoided drawing conclusions and instead simply reported the probability that particular claims were true. In that way, the scientists would not need to make decisions about what errors were most important to avoid; by reporting probabilities, they could let others choose how much evidence to demand before drawing conclusions. According to another objection, which Douglas (2009) attributes to Isaac Levi (1960), scientists should take only epistemic considerations into account when making judgements in the face of inductive risk.[15] According to this view, the scientific community has its own standards of evidence or 'canons of inference' that are independent of broader social considerations. This perspective accords well with another point made by Jeffrey (1956), which is that there are so many different potential consequences associated with accepting or rejecting a hypothesis that it would be a mistake for scientists to try to take these consequences into account when doing their work.

---

[14] One would need to revise the details of the error argument slightly to accommodate other epistemic risks in addition to inductive risks. For example, rather than arguing that values are necessary to decide how to handle the risks of drawing false-positive versus false-negative conclusions (as in the case of the original error argument), a broadened form of the error argument would need to argue that values are necessary to decide how to manage other risks as well (e.g., the risks of obscuring various kinds of information). Although some of these risks might not count as errors in the sense of inferring false facts, Harvard and Winsberg (2021) argue that they are errors in a different sense: they involve representational decisions that are inadequate for their purposes.

[15] I have formulated Levi's objection in accordance with Douglas's interpretation of it. Others have suggested that Levi is focused primarily on arguing that all scientists can employ the same standards of evidence in the same situations and that he does not focus on whether those standards of evidence incorporate epistemic or non-epistemic considerations (see, e.g., Boulicault and Schroeder 2021; Staley 2017). This alternative interpretation of Levi has much in common with the view taken by John (2015b), which is discussed later in this section. Regardless of what view Levi actually held, the objection that Douglas attributes to him is important to consider.

These objections do not appear to be compelling, however. Rudner (1953) himself anticipated Jeffrey's objection and argued that even when scientists make probability estimates, they are still drawing conclusions about those probabilities, which means they still face decisions that incorporate inductive risk (see, e.g., Steele 2012). And with respect to Levi's objection, Douglas (2017) argues that it is unrealistic and unethical to try to set standards of evidence in science without some consideration of non-epistemic factors. She emphasises that there are no a priori reasons why scientists should choose one standard of evidence rather than another solely on epistemic grounds; the nature of epistemic considerations is to provide evidence for hypotheses, not to assess what level of evidence is sufficient (Douglas 2017, 2021). From a purely epistemic perspective, scientists could just as well set a 90 per cent or a 99 per cent statistical significance level as opposed to a 95 per cent statistical significance level. Scientific communities can, of course, choose particular standards of evidence as a matter of convention (Wilholt 2009), but those conventions vary across different scientific fields. Given scientists' moral responsibilities not to act recklessly or negligently, it would be irresponsible for them to ignore the social context of their work when setting those conventions (Douglas 2017).

The objections associated with the work of Jeffrey and Levi have been adapted and extended by other thinkers, however. For example, Gregor Betz (2013, 2017) argues that scientists can avoid the value-laden judgements involved in responding to inductive risk if they draw conclusions only when they are beyond reasonable doubt. He contends that if a conclusion is so certain that there is essentially no inductive risk when making it, then scientists do not have a responsibility to incorporate non-epistemic values in their reasoning when drawing the conclusion. It might seem unrealistic that scientists could avoid making claims that are uncertain, but Betz (2013) suggests that they can do so by strategically 'hedging' or weakening their claims. For example, rather than claiming that climate change will have a particular effect or that the effect has a particular probability of occurring, one could simply say that the effect is possible. Betz contends that if scientists weaken their claims enough, they can make claims that are reasonably certain.

Another strategy that scientists can use to hedge their claims is to state all the value-laden judgements associated with them. For example, Betz suggests that scientists could make claims that run something like this: 'Given these non-epistemic value judgements (which we have used to fill the inferential gaps we faced because of substantial uncertainties) we arrive at the following findings: . . .' (2017, 104). In other words, scientists would face inductive risk if they simply reported their findings, but they can potentially avoid this inductive risk by making the more careful claim that *if* one made particular value-laden judgements, *then* one would arrive at particular findings. Like Jeffrey's strategy of providing probabilities, this approach essentially 'defers' decisions under inductive risk to decision-makers. The decision-makers who received this hedged information would have to decide whether or not they felt comfortable accepting the conclusions that were based on particular value-laden judgements or whether they wanted to make different judgements (see Havstad and Brown 2017).

Betz's critique of the error argument faces challenges of its own, however. Perhaps the greatest worry is that scientists would be much less helpful to decision-makers if they were forced to hedge all their claims to the point that they were reasonably certain (Elliott 2011b; Frank 2017). If scientists were to follow the hedging strategy of avoiding specific predictions and instead offering only general conclusions that were certain beyond any reasonable doubt, pol-icymakers would be forced to make many of their decisions in a state of significant scientific uncertainty. Admittedly, there are frameworks for deci-sion-making under uncertainty (Betz 2017), but many policymakers would probably prefer for scientists to provide them with somewhat more specific predictions, even if they were fallible, rather than leaving them with extremely vague claims about a host of potential threats and opportunities.[16]

Betz's other hedging strategy (namely, having scientists clarify all the value-laden judgements associated with their conclusions) is also likely to be unhelp-ful in many cases. As Havstad and Brown (2017) emphasise, scientists often face an enormous number of methodological and interpretive decisions throughout their work. For example, consider some of the judgements involved in making predictions on the basis of climate models:

> Such choices might include decisions about different possible parameteriza-tions and model structures, particular parameter values, choice [sic] between different approximation methods, decisions about which climate forcings to include in the model or exclude as insignificant or approximate with a simple parameter, choice of higher or lower model resolution (or grid size), decisions about aggregating ensembles of models, and so on.
>
> (Havstad and Brown 2017, 112)

It seems unrealistic to expect scientists to keep track of all these decisions and report them and their implications to decision-makers. And even if they could

---

[16] Of course, there are more and less responsible ways of providing predictions to policymakers in the face of significant scientific uncertainty. If scientists decide to make specific predictions under such circumstances, it is typically important for them to clarify that they are making fallible predictions that could very well turn out to be incorrect.

achieve this, the attempt to explain all these judgements to decision-makers would likely be overwhelming and confusing (Elliott 2011b). Thus, Betz's recommendation for scientists to hedge their claims and to avoid making uncertain claims faces significant challenges.

Stephen John (2015b) provides a somewhat different response to the error argument. He contends that even if scientists do need to take the social consequences of error into account, the most profound social consequence they need to consider is the trust and confidence that the public has in the scientific community. Moreover, he argues that if scientists were to regularly change their standards of evidence when drawing conclusions for the public under various circumstances, it would leave the public unsure about how much confidence to maintain towards scientists' claims. Therefore, he concludes that it is best for scientists to maintain a fixed, high standard of evidence so that everyone knows what to expect.[17]

John's argument provides a valuable reminder that there are social costs to allowing scientists to vary their standards of evidence, but one can acknowledge his concerns without fully sharing his conclusion that scientists should hold their standards of evidence fixed. After all, scientists already employ different standards of evidence in different fields (Douglas 2017). Thus, it is clearly possible to have some variation in scientific standards of evidence without causing a problematic amount of public confusion. Moreover, in some areas of enquiry, such as when scientists are studying environmental threats to local communities, there might be very severe social consequences associated with demanding high standards of evidence before concluding that threats are present. It might very well be better for scientists to lower their standards of evidence in such cases (and be clear about the fact that they are lowering them) than to maintain high standards of evidence just because of an abstract concern for maintaining public confidence in science (Boulicault and Schroeder 2021). Thus, even though John is probably correct that there are benefits to establishing conventional standards of evidence, it is doubtful that scientists must rigidly follow the same standards in all cases. At the very least, his objection requires much more empirical and ethical discussion regarding the effects on public trust of varying scientific standards of evidence in different contexts (see, e.g., Elliott et al. 2017).

---

[17] As discussed in footnote 15, Levi (1960) may have actually held a view close to John's, according to which scientific reasoning can achieve a form of value-freedom or value-neutrality in the sense that individual scientists do not make idiosyncratic judgements distinct from the standard canons of inference held by all scientists (see, e.g., Boulicault and Schroeder 2021; Staley 2017). My response to John could be employed in response to this interpretation of Levi as well.

3.4 The Aims Argument

A third argument for incorporating non-epistemic values in scientific reasoning focuses on the aims of research. (See Table 3 for an overview of this argument and the debates concerning it.) In many contexts, scientists have non-epistemic aims that go beyond merely arriving at true or reliable information about the world. As a result, proponents of the aims argument contend that it is necessary for scientists to employ non-epistemic values in their reasoning so that they can achieve their non-epistemic aims. For example, as mentioned in Section 2, Kristen Intemann (2015) points out that climate modellers have to make difficult choices when deciding how to optimise their models. To handle these decisions responsibly, she argues that the modellers need to consider their overarching aim of generating the information that matters most to those who use the models. Thus, modellers need to incorporate the non-epistemic values of those who use their models when evaluating the models' quality.

Similarly, Daniel McKaughan and I have argued that when scientists do research that informs the work of government regulatory agencies, they need to consider the aims of those agencies (Elliott and McKaughan 2014; see also Fernández Pinto and Hicks 2019). Those agencies typically care not only about the accuracy of the information they receive but also about whether that information can be generated efficiently, affordably, and in a manner they can

Table 3 A brief overview of the aims argument, together with a major objection and responses to it

Argument	Objection	Responses
In order to achieve the non-epistemic aims of science, scientists need to take non-epistemic values into account when assessing the quality of scientific models, hypotheses, and theories (see, e.g., Intemann 2015).	Some non-epistemic aims for science may be inappropriate (Steel 2017).	Questionable aims can be managed through transparency (Elliott and McKaughan 2014). Aims can be evaluated to determine whether they are appropriate (Hicks 2014). Basic epistemic constraints can limit the problematic effects of questionable aims (Steel 2017).

use effectively to accomplish their missions. In some cases, it might be more important for these agencies to receive standardised information that is relatively quick and easy to produce than to receive the most accurate information possible. For example, with thousands of industrial chemicals in use, it might be better for a regulatory agency to use a scientific method that can estimate the safety of those chemicals quickly rather than for the agency to use a slightly more accurate method that takes an enormous amount of time, money, and effort (Elliott and McKaughan 2014). Thus, scientific models, methods, and hypotheses sometimes need to be evaluated not only in terms of their epistemic characteristics but also based on non-epistemic considerations.

Perhaps the fundamental concern with this argument, however, is that not all aims for science are appropriate. Thus, it seems problematic to 'unleash' scientists to assess scientific models or hypotheses based on any non-epistemic values that support their aims. Daniel Steel (2017) makes this point in a particularly striking way by referring to Henrik Ibsen's play, *An Enemy of the People*, which recounts the story of a doctor who is driven out of his town because he discovers and tries to publicise the finding that the town's economically valuable baths are contaminated. Steel argues that the kind of situation described by Ibsen occurs relatively frequently when scientific researchers discover that economically valuable resources or activities (e.g., tobacco smoking, lead, pesticides, fossil fuels, pharmaceuticals, plastics, and so on) have harmful effects on human health or the environment (see, e.g., McGarity and Wagner 2008; Michaels 2008; Oreskes and Conway 2010). Steel (2017) argues that the aims approach runs into serious problems in the face of these 'Ibsen predicaments'. For example, suppose that a pharmaceutical company had the aim of maximising its profits, even if that required denying serious side effects associated with its drugs. On the aims approach, it would seem appropriate for the company to do whatever it took to achieve that aim, even if it involved ignoring evidence, deliberately designing studies to obtain preferred results, and interpreting data in questionable ways for the sake of defending its drugs.

This is a serious concern, but it is probably not fatal for the aims approach. As Steel (2017) himself acknowledges, there are strategies for getting around his worries. One option is to insist that researchers need to be open and transparent about their aims and the value-laden judgements they have made in order to achieve those aims (Elliott and McKaughan 2014). However, achieving transparency of this sort is not a simple matter (Elliott 2020b, 2021); it is not clear that scientists can consistently achieve the level of transparency needed to make this solution work (John 2018; Steel 2017). Another option is to call for thoughtful ethical and political reflection to determine what aims are appropriate in particular scientific contexts (see, e.g., Fernández Pinto and Hicks 2019; Hicks 2014; Intemann 2015); with this strategy, one could try to ensure that scientists pursue only acceptable aims. Of course, the difficulty with this solution is that ethical and political reflection is fraught with uncertainty and the potential for disagreement. A third option is to limit the aims argument by adding some basic epistemic constraints that scientists must respect, no matter what their aims might be (see, e.g., Steel 2017). For example, one might argue that it is never acceptable for scientists to fabricate or falsify their data. By adding constraints like these, one might be able to accept the aims approach while avoiding the worst abuses that worried Steel.

3.5 The Conceptual Argument

A fourth argument for incorporating non-epistemic values in scientific reasoning focuses on the conceptual categories employed in scientific research. (Table 4 provides an overview of this section's discussion of the conceptual argument.) According to this argument, the concepts employed in at least some areas of science actually blend epistemic and non-epistemic content, so both epistemic and non-epistemic values are relevant to assessing hypotheses that incorporate these concepts. Anna Alexandrova (2018) argues that many hypotheses in the social sciences have this sort of 'mixed' character. She defines a mixed hypothesis as one that makes an empirical claim but that also incorporates one or more variables that require non-epistemic value judgements in order to define them (Alexandrova 2018). For example, consider the hypothesis that long commutes between one's home and work are associated with lower human well-being. Alexandrova argues that the concept of well-being can be defined in a number of different ways and that deciding which concept is best requires

Table 4 A brief overview of the conceptual argument, together with major objections and responses

Argument	Objections	Responses
Non-epistemic values are relevant to assessing scientific hypotheses that incorporate 'mixed' or value-laden concepts (see, e.g., Alexandrova 2018).	Mixed or value-laden concepts should be eliminated to the extent feasible. Value-laden decisions about mixed concepts can be deferred to decision-makers.	Eliminating mixed and value-laden concepts would impoverish science (Dupré 2007). Deferring all decisions about mixed concepts is unrealistic (Alexandrova 2018).

judgements that involve non-epistemic values. Therefore, one cannot assess whether long commutes are associated with lower well-being without making non-epistemic value judgements about how to define the central concept at issue.[18]

Although one might think that value-laden concepts are found primarily in the social sciences, they appear to be surprisingly widespread. For example, David Ludwig (2016) contends that hypotheses involving a wide array of concepts (e.g., species, race, memory, and intelligence) end up incorporating non-epistemic value judgements because they require ontological choices. For instance, hypotheses about the number of species in a given location require decisions about which of several different possible species concepts to employ. Ludwig argues that in many cases, these ontological choices are based on non-epistemic considerations about which concepts best serve our practical interests (see also Brigandt 2020).

I have made the related argument that concepts and categories across a wide array of scientific disciplines are value-laden in the sense that choosing which concepts or categories to employ has implications for how people think about and respond to scientific issues (Elliott 2017). In the field of toxicology, for example, researchers have noticed that referring to chemicals as 'endocrine disruptors' is more emotionally charged and suggestive of harm than speaking of 'hormonally active agents', and they have debated which concept is more appropriate to employ (Elliott 2009). Similarly, as mentioned previously in this Element, researchers face difficult decisions about whether or not to employ racial categories in medicine because the use of those categories can have significant social consequences. On one hand, the use of racial categories can promote misleading views about the biological reality of race, but on the other hand, the use of racial categories can help highlight the presence of health disparities caused by social inequities (Elliott 2017). In the environmental sciences, researchers employ a wide array of metaphorical concepts that carry both positive and negative connotations associated with the social contexts from which they originated (e.g., 'biodiversity', 'invasive species', 'competition', 'ecological integrity', and 'natural capital'; Elliott 2020a; Larson 2011). In all these cases, scientists arguably have a responsibility to bring non-epistemic values to bear when choosing their concepts and categories because the available options all have social ramifications that need to be considered.

It is worth noting, however, that there are two slightly different ways of formulating this conceptual argument against the value-free ideal. One version

---

[18] For another very thoughtful discussion of the roles that non-epistemic values play in the use of scientific concepts, see Dupré (2007).

focuses on the social ramifications of using one concept or category rather than another one. According to this version of the argument, scientists have the responsibility to employ non-epistemic values in the course of assessing those ramifications and deciding which concepts are the most socially responsible to employ. For example, one might conclude that scientists should employ racial categories only under carefully circumscribed conditions when the benefits for those who have been disadvantaged by those categories appear to outweigh the potential harms. A second version of the conceptual argument focuses on the intrinsic justifiability of particular concepts. For example, when Alexandrova (2018) calls for the use of non-epistemic values in assessing which concept of human well-being to employ, she does not appear to be focused primarily on assessing the social consequences of choosing one concept or another but rather on deciding what concept actually captures human well-being best.

It might not always be easy to distinguish these two different formulations of the conceptual argument, but the difference between them is significant because the second formulation supports a deeper critique of the value-free ideal. The first formulation shows that non-epistemic values sometimes play an ethically necessary role in scientific reasoning, insofar as scientists have a responsibility not to cause reckless or negligent harm to others (Douglas 2009). The second formulation supports the deeper claim that non-epistemic values actually enhance scientific reasoning. This formulation is significant because at least some figures suggest that a truly convincing critique of the value-free ideal ought to show not only that non-epistemic values are a 'necessary evil' in scientific reasoning (i.e., they sometimes need to be used when dealing with scientific uncertainty) but also that non-epistemic values are actually desirable or beneficial for scientific reasoning (see de Melo-Martín and Intemann 2016). According to the second formulation of the conceptual argument, some fields of science employ concepts that incorporate both empirical and normative components, and so good scientific reasoning requires that scientists appeal at least in part to non-epistemic values when assessing hypotheses in those fields of science.

Of course, there are still various strategies available for trying to counter the conceptual argument. One option would be to insist that scientists should strive to identify value-laden concepts and replace them or redefine them to eliminate any normative components. However, Dupré (2007) points out that this would impoverish scientific practice. He argues that for the social sciences to be useful, they need to employ concepts that reflect social practices and experiences, and those concepts are often laden with non-epistemic values. Alternatively, one could resist the conceptual argument by employing the same kinds of 'deferral' strategies suggested in response to the error argument. For example, scientists could employ hypothetical claims like 'If one employs such-and-such a conception of well-being, then long commutes between one's home and work are associated with lower well-being'. As in the case of the error argument, however, it is doubtful that these efforts at deferral can consistently succeed. For example, as Alexandrova (2018) points out, it would be unrealistic for scientists to discuss every possible conception of well-being, and thus, they are forced to make implicit judgements about which conceptions are most compelling and thus worth discussing. Furthermore, I have argued that once one starts to consider all the social ramifications of employing different scientific concepts, a vast array of scientific concepts end up being value-laden to at least some extent. Therefore, in many cases, there are likely to be no value-neutral concepts available; scientists will have to choose some concepts over others, and by doing so, they will be implicitly choosing to prioritise some non-epistemic values over others (Elliott 2017, 13).

3.6 Moving Forward

These debates about whether to deliberately incorporate non-epistemic values in scientific reasoning are obviously complex, but the arguments discussed throughout this section suggest several lessons that can guide future work on these issues. The first lesson is that it is crucial to appreciate the differences between different fields of science and the different contexts in which science is used; the strengths of the objections and responses to the gap, error, aims, and conceptual arguments vary significantly depending on the details of the context in which they are employed. For example, the gap argument is likely to be most compelling in contexts where it is problematic for scientists to withhold their judgement and wait until they have compelling empirical evidence for their background assumptions. Similarly, the cogency of Betz's objections to the error argument depends on the nature of the case under consideration. For example, David Frank (2017) has proposed a set of conditions that determine whether scientists can present carefully hedged representations of uncertainty for decision-makers or whether it is better for them to make their own value-laden judgements in response to inductive risk. When decision-makers are able to understand representations of uncertainty, when scientists are unlikely to manipulate those representations for political ends, and when those representations have been produced with well-established methods that leave little higher-order uncertainty, Frank contends that scientists are better able to defer value-laden decisions to others. In other cases, the error argument poses a more powerful threat to the value-free ideal. And, of course, the aims and conceptual arguments depend on the notions that some fields of science have non-epistemic aims or employ mixed concepts; if non-epistemic aims or mixed concepts are minimal in some fields of science, then roles for non-epistemic values will be correspondingly limited.[19]

A second lesson for moving forward is that it would be fruitful to think more carefully about how to divide up the responsibility for handling value-laden judgements between individual scientists and scientific institutions. John (2015b) makes this point particularly well in his response to the error argument. He emphasises that even if one acknowledges that value-laden judgements must be made when drawing scientific conclusions, it does not mean that one must leave the responsibility for making those judgements to individual scientists. One might conclude that the most responsible way to handle such decisions is to turn them over to larger scientific institutions to decide how to make them. Building on John's argument, one might think that scientific societies or other organisations should deliberate about the most responsible ways to handle value judgements, and then individual scientists should abide by those conventions (Wilholt 2009). This strategy could be used for handling a wide array of different value-laden judgements in science. For example, the Organisation for Economic Cooperation and Development (OECD) sets guidelines for how to perform many scientific studies for regulatory purposes (Elliott 2016). Many of these guidelines are value-laden (i.e., there is no compelling empirical reason to make them one way rather than another, and they have significant social consequences). Nevertheless, it might seem best to leave these value-laden decisions with the OECD rather than with individual scientists. Thus, it is important for philosophers of science to think further about when it is best to handle values at an institutional level and when it is better to handle them at an individual level. They also need to consider when to let individual scientists deviate from institutional standards and how to communicate appropriately about those deviations (de Winter 2016).

Building on these first two lessons, another important lesson is that not all value-laden judgements need to be handled in the same way, even within the same research programme. Scientists could follow advice from proponents of the value-free ideal in some cases and critics of the value-free ideal in other cases. For example, given that scientists are often forced to make a large number of methodological and interpretive judgements in the course of their work, it seems unrealistic to expect them to pursue a strategy that requires deferring *all* of those judgements to decision-makers (Havstad and Brown 2017). Nevertheless, this does not mean that they should never defer *any* of them.

---

[19] It is important to remember that there are multiple ways to formulate the conceptual argument, however. Even if some fields of science do not employ mixed concepts, those fields might still employ concepts or categories that have important impacts on society. Thus, there might still be roles for non-epistemic values in deciding which concepts or categories to employ.

For instance, even if scientists working on a particular research project were forced to make a number of judgements that inclined their conclusions in one direction or another (in accordance with the error argument), they might decide that one or two of their judgements were so significant that they should defer them to others as Betz suggests. In such cases, they could tell decision-makers that the available evidence is consistent with more than one interpretation and discuss the considerations for and against those interpretations (Elliott and Richards 2017b, 269). Thus, scientists can incorporate non-epistemic values in some aspects of their reasoning while still adopting strategies to limit roles for non-epistemic values in other aspects of their reasoning.

A fourth lesson is that once the critics and the proponents of the value-free ideal nuance their views in response to each other's arguments, their views are often not as far apart as they might initially appear. Consider, for example, disagreements over how to respond to the error argument. In order to avoid drawing value-laden conclusions, Betz (2017) suggests that scientists can hedge their claims by saying that *if* one were to make particular value-laden judgements, *then* one would arrive at particular conclusions. This approach is ultimately not so different from the one taken by many proponents of the error argument, who claim that scientists should try to be transparent or open about the value-laden judgements they have made (see, e.g., Douglas 2008; Elliott and Resnik 2014; Stanev 2017). Both the opponents and the proponents of the error argument often claim that it is important for scientists to clarify the value-laden judgements involved in their reasoning. The opponents just think scientists should try to specify the judgements that *could* be made so that others can make them instead, whereas the proponents think it is often more practical for scientists to make the judgements themselves while still making efforts to clarify them to the extent that they can.

Another way to bring the views of the critics and the proponents of the value-free ideal closer together is to clarify the different cognitive attitudes on which they focus (see, e.g., McKaughan and Elliott 2015). Scientists' cognitive attitudes are the evaluative responses they take towards content like hypotheses, theories, or models. For example, scientists could *believe* a hypothesis to be true, but they could also *entertain* it or *presuppose* it or *judge it to be worthy of further investigation* (McKaughan and Elliott 2015). When defenders of the value-free ideal challenge appeals to non-epistemic values based on the contention that those values do not provide evidence for the truth of theories or hypotheses (e.g., McMullin 1983), they are affirming that non-epistemic values are irrelevant to the cognitive attitude of belief. But critics of the value-free ideal can agree with its defenders on this point and instead focus on other cognitive attitudes. For example, David Willmes and I have argued that scientists frequently *accept* hypotheses for practical purposes, and it often makes sense for non-epistemic values to influence those practical decisions (Elliott and Willmes 2013). Similarly, Marina DiMarco and Kareem Khalifa (2019) emphasise that scientists are often engaged in *pursuing* particular hypotheses because of non-epistemic values. If one took a pragmatic attitude towards the practice of science, one might conclude that scientists are almost always engaged in pursuing or accepting hypotheses for various practical purposes rather than believing them. Thus, some of the seemingly conflicting advice coming from critics and defenders of the value-free ideal could potentially be alleviated by distinguishing different cognitive attitudes that scientists employ and clarifying that non-epistemic values are more relevant to some of those cognitive attitudes than others (see, e.g., DiMarco and Khalifa 2019; Elliott 2017; Lacey 2017).

A final lesson, assuming one accepts the conclusion that values should at least sometimes be deliberately incorporated into scientific reasoning, is that further efforts are needed to manage these values responsibly. As Steel (2017) argued in response to the aims argument, it seems problematic to give scientists free rein to pursue any aims they want. Instead, efforts are needed to clarify which aims are appropriate and how best to handle conflicts between epistemic aims and non-epistemic aims. The same point applies to the gap, error, and conceptual arguments; not all value influences are equally acceptable. For example, Intemann (2005) emphasises that scientists need to reflect on which values are relevant to filling the evidential gaps they face. Similarly, Douglas (2009) argues that scientists need to consider their moral responsibilities when deciding which values to prioritise when weighing the potential consequences of false-positive and false-negative errors. In the same way, I argue that scientists ought to engage in ethical reflection and consultation with stakeholders to decide how to handle conceptual choices in science (Elliott 2009). Thus, to abandon the value-free ideal is not to call for a free-for-all in which values of all sorts are accepted in every part of science. We need strategies for managing these values and considering which values are appropriate in which cases. That is the question to which we turn in Section 4 of this Element.

4 How Can We Manage Values in Science Responsibly?

When reflecting on the best ways to manage values in science, it is important to remember the full range of ways they can intersect with scientific practice, as discussed in Section 2. Values can relate not only to the judgements involved in scientific reasoning (as discussed in Section 3) but also to the judgements involved in choosing scientific projects, interacting with other scientists, and using science for making decisions. Nevertheless, this Element focuses especially on managing values in scientific reasoning because the contemporary literature in the philosophy of science revolves primarily around that issue. There are other academic fields (e.g., studies of research ethics, responsible innovation, anticipatory governance, and risk management) that delve deeply into strategies for managing values in other aspects of science. Still, as I argue later in the Element, it would be a mistake to ignore these other aspects of science entirely. As Section 2 emphasised, the ways values intersect with one category of science can affect other categories of science as well, so it is important to keep all aspects of science in mind even while focusing on managing values in scientific reasoning. This section will explore the strengths and weaknesses of four major proposals for managing values in this aspect of science. Building on these previous accounts, Section 5 will sketch out avenues for exploring this issue in future philosophical work.

4.1 Choosing the Right Values

Perhaps the most obvious and straightforward way to manage values in scientific reasoning is to insist that science should be influenced only by the *right* values. Nevertheless, there are different ways of determining which values count as the right ones. One way is to argue that those values should be determined through ethical reasoning. Janet Kourany (2010) and Matt Brown (2020) are two of the most influential advocates of this approach. Kourany argues for replacing the value-free ideal with the ideal of 'socially responsible science', according to which 'sound social values as well as sound epistemic values must control every aspect of the scientific research process' (Kourany 2013, 93–4). Her vision for implementing this ideal is to develop thoughtful ethics codes for each field of science in order to guide scientists in making appropriate judgements throughout the research enterprise. Brown suggests a somewhat similar approach, which he calls the ideal of moral imagination: '*Scientists should recognize the contingencies in their work as unforced choices, discover morally salient aspects of the situation they are deciding, empathetically recognize and understand the legitimate stakeholders, imaginatively construct and explore possible options, and exercise fair and warranted value judgment in order to guide those decisions*' (Brown 2020, 21, italics in original). In order to implement this approach, he focuses more on ethical reasoning by individual scientists as opposed to Kourany's emphasis on ethics codes, but both approaches clearly focus on helping scientists make choices that accord with the most ethically justifiable values (see also Hicks 2014).

It is undoubtedly important to make sure that the values incorporated into science are ethically justifiable. Nevertheless, this approach runs into difficulties. Perhaps the most significant problem is that ethical reasoning is notoriously difficult and contested. Even though figures like Anderson (2004), Brown (2020), and Clough and Loges (2008) emphasise that we can draw on empirical evidence to help determine which values are most justifiable, ethical reasoning is still typically underdetermined by the available evidence and subject to deep disagreements.[20] Thus, when scientists are dealing with complicated judgements that pit multiple important values against each other, it is likely to be very difficult to decide which value judgements are the most ethically justifiable (Holman and Wilholt 2022).

A related worry is that it could be difficult to employ this approach in practice. Even though Brown (2020) provides guidance to help scientists identify important issues to think about, most scientists are still unlikely to have the training necessary to engage in deep ethical reflection about their value judgements. Thus, even though it would be beneficial to encourage them to reflect more carefully on the ethical ramifications of their choices, it would probably be unwise to depend on them to arrive at the best conclusions by themselves. Kourany addresses this worry to some extent by relying on ethics codes rather than the ethical judgements of individual scientists; ethics codes can be developed using an interdisciplinary approach that draws on the strengths of multiple disciplines (Kourany 2013). Nevertheless, most complex ethical scenarios are likely to pit multiple ethical principles against each other, so scientists are still likely to be forced to engage in difficult judgements about how to interpret and prioritise the principles found in ethics codes.

Andrew Schroeder (2021, 2022) suggests a somewhat different version of the 'right values' approach that might help address some of these worries. Rather than arriving at the right values through *ethical* reasoning, he focuses on *political* reasoning (see also Intemann 2015; Kitcher 2001; Lusk 2020). In other words, he draws on principles from political philosophy, which is commonly regarded to be distinct from ethics in that it is designed specifically to help us 'establish common rules for a society marked by disagreement about values' and 'balance people's conflicting rights and liberties' (Schroeder 2020, 2).[21] On this basis, he argues that scientific reasoning should be guided by the values that are representative of the population. There are obviously a range of complex issues involved in deciding which values are

---

[20] For the purposes of this Element, I am setting aside difficult metaethical questions about the extent to which empirical evidence is relevant to assessing claims about ethics and values. My point is that even if one grants that empirical evidence is relevant, the evidence is still typically insufficient to resolve ethical disputes.

[21] I am following Schroeder (2020) in distinguishing ethical and political reasoning. According to some views, political reasoning could ultimately be grounded in or reduced to ethical reasoning.

actually representative of the population, but Schroeder suggests that political philosophy can help us work through these issues. In some cases, it might be best to engage in a deliberative exercise to elicit the public's values, whereas, in other cases, one might be able to appeal to surveys or other empirical data. At any rate, Schroeder argues that this proposal preserves the trustworthiness of science because decision-makers can be confident that different scientists will arrive at roughly the same conclusions, and those conclusions will be based on 'objective facts plus democratic values' (Schroeder 2021, 555).

Although this political approach is promising in some respects, it faces at least three worries of its own. The first worry is that some populations might accept values that are ethically repugnant or based on empirical falsehoods. For example, as discussed at the beginning of this Element, science has historically been influenced by racist values, and as a result, many historically disadvantaged groups continue to distrust the scientific community. Schroeder (2022) has a promising response to this worry, though; he argues that the democratic values espoused by a population can be 'filtered' and 'laundered' to remove values that are obviously problematic (see also Kitcher 2001).

The other two worries associated with the political approach may be cause for greater concern, however. The second worry is that it is not always clear which 'population' is the relevant one to examine when trying to arrive at democratic values. Should one focus on the entire global population, or the population of a particular country or region, or those who will be most affected by the science being done, or some other group? This question is not always easy to answer, and it can have a significant impact on the values that emerge from Schroeder's recommended political exercise.

The third worry associated with the political approach is that there are so many judgements that pervade scientific research that it would be difficult to engage in a political procedure to determine which values should inform all these judgements. To be fair to Schroeder, one might be able to group these judgements into categories (e.g., judgements involving the discount rate in economics, the labelling of diseases, toxicity testing for industrial chemicals, the estimation of disability-adjusted life years in health policy, integrated assessment models for climate modelling, and so on).One could then engage in a political procedure to determine which non-epistemic values are applicable to each general category rather than trying to determine the values appropriate to each individual judgement. Nevertheless, this categorisation scheme could fall prey to a dilemma. If the categories were made very broad, then it would be unlikely that the values assigned to each category would actually be appropriate for all the judgements within each category. If the categories were made narrow enough to solve this problem, however, the effort involved in identifying the democratic values applicable to all those categories would likely be overwhelming. Thus, Schroeder's political proposal could be extremely valuable in a limited number of cases where there is a great deal of interest in pursuing political procedures to identify the democratic values that should guide particular judgements, but it might not be practical for addressing the entirety of judgements that pervade scientific research.

Another view about what constitutes the 'right' values for a scientific research project is that they should be the values of those who will be making use of the research.[22] In other words, one could strive to 'align' (Schroeder 2021) or 'coordinate' (Holman and Wilholt 2022) the values used by scientists with the interests of the users of that science. For example, Parker and Lusk (2019) recommend this approach for climate services organisations that advise communities about the future effects of climate change. As discussed in Section 2, Parker and Lusk (2019) point out that these organisations are forced to make numerous judgements (e.g., about which models to use, how to combine information from multiple models, and how to estimate the uncertainty around their predictions) in the course of their work. They suggest that these organisations should try to handle these judgements in a way that accords with the values of those they are serving.

Like the ethical and political approaches to identifying the right values, this approach has its strengths and weaknesses. It works best in cases where scientists are working with a relatively homogeneous set of decision-makers who share the same values and who can inform scientists about their priorities. For example, as discussed earlier in this Element, many scientists working in fields like environmental health are striving to engage in CBPR, in which they collaborate with specific communities to shape their research in ways that meet the needs and concerns of those communities (e.g., Claudio 2000). Nevertheless, this approach is relatively unhelpful when research is not being done on behalf of a specific community or set of decision-makers. Moreover, Schroeder (2021) worries that this approach could promote social polarisation, with different interest groups generating and appealing to science guided by their preferred values. Finally, this approach could also generate ethical quandaries for scientists who strongly disagree with the values held by specific communities (Schroeder 2017), although one could presumably develop principles for navigating these conflicts.

---

[22] Lusk (2020) argues that the approach of employing the values associated with the specific users of research is ultimately compatible with the political approach described by Schroeder.

4.2 Choosing the Right Roles for Values

Another strategy for managing values in scientific reasoning is to specify specific roles or functions for values that are acceptable and unacceptable.[23] Heather Douglas (2009) presents a particularly influential version of this strategy as part of her discussion of the error argument. She distinguishes a 'direct' role for values from an 'indirect' role. When values play a direct role, they act as 'warrant or reasons to accept a claim' (2009, 96), whereas in the indirect role they 'act to weigh the importance of uncertainty, helping to decide what should count as *sufficient*' evidence for a choice (2009, 96, emphasis in original). She argues that it would be problematic for values to play a direct role in scientific reasoning when scientists are examining the evidence for their conclusions; to do so would be to fall prey to 'wishful thinking', accepting claims just because they fit with one's preferences (Douglas 2009, 96). However, she insists that values can legitimately play indirect roles in scientific reasoning by helping scientists decide how much evidence they should demand before drawing conclusions. She also emphasises that values can legitimately play a direct role in other aspects of research, such as steering, managing, or using research (see Section 2).

A significant strength of this approach is that it maintains a clear distinction between factors that count as evidence from those that do not. This helps address a worry about approaches that focus instead on getting the 'right' values, namely that they could end up allowing scientists to wield values in ways that do not make sense. Even if a value is well justified, it might just not be relevant for some purposes. For example, even though egalitarian values are ethically justified, it does not necessarily mean that a particular theory receives evidential support from the fact that it supports egalitarian values. Douglas avoids this problem by clarifying the cognitive roles for which values are relevant from those for which they are not.

Unfortunately, Douglas's approach also runs into complications. One worry is that the distinction between direct and indirect roles might not be as clear as it initially appears. For example, in addition to the ways of distinguishing direct and indirect roles discussed previously, Douglas also assumes that when values act in the indirect role, they involve *unintended* consequences associated with errors, whereas when values act in a direct role, they involve *intended*

---

[23] An important question to keep in mind is whether the various strategies discussed in Section 4 for managing values are mutually exclusive or whether they could be employed together. Douglas appeared to argue in some of her earlier work that values could be managed adequately by focusing on the right roles for values (e.g., Douglas 2009). In contrast, I suggest later in this Element that it might be best to combine multiple approaches, and Douglas appears to be leaning in that direction as well in her more recent work (see, e.g., Douglas 2021).

consequences that scientists aim to achieve (2009, 96). However, it is at least logically possible that scientists could be thinking about the intended consequences that they aim to achieve (which sounds like the direct role) when they weigh the importance of uncertainty and decide how much evidence is sufficient for drawing conclusions (which sounds like the indirect role; Elliott 2013; Elliott and Richards 2017b, 266). And even if this conceptual ambiguity were cleared up, it might still be difficult for scientists to implement this distinction in practice. For example, when scientists choose particular analytical techniques or models or interpretations of the available evidence because of particular values (e.g., concern for public health), it might be unclear even in the scientists' own minds whether those values were influencing them directly (because they wanted to bring about a particular outcome) or indirectly (because they were concerned about the consequences of error; see, e.g., Bluhm 2017; Elliott 2011a, 321).

Another important worry about the distinction between direct and indirect roles is that it might not be sufficient to prevent problematic influences of values on scientific reasoning. For example, Daniel Steel and Kyle Whyte (2012) challenge Douglas's distinction by considering the case of a hypothetical pharmaceutical corporation that must consider how to handle the uncertainties associated with its clinical trials. Steel and Whyte imagine a scenario in which the company, whether because of concerns about profits or concerns about the harmful social impact of keeping potentially beneficial drugs off the market, decides to demand an especially high standard of evidence before accepting and publicising evidence about the harmful side effects of its products. Even if values were playing an indirect role in a case like this, Steel and Whyte argue that it would constitute a problematic influence of values on scientific reasoning.[24]

To address cases like this, Steel and Whyte propose a different limitation on the roles that values play in scientific reasoning. They propose a 'values-in-science standard', according to which 'nonepistemic values should not conflict with epistemic values in the design, interpretation, or dissemination of scientific research that is practically feasible and ethically permissible' (2012, 169). This view has much in common with the gap argument discussed in Section 3, insofar as it allows non-epistemic values to influence science only when

---

[24] Douglas could potentially respond to this objection by supplementing her focus on the right *roles* for values with some additional constraints involving the right *kinds* of values. So, for example, she could argue on ethical or political grounds that it would be problematic for a company to put so much emphasis on their profits at the expense of public health. Along these lines, I argue later in this Element for an approach that combines different strategies for managing values. I thank Drew Schroeder for helping me clarify this point.

epistemic considerations leave researchers with multiple options that are equally well supported by the available evidence. However, this approach may still run into difficulties because it is not always clear how to identify cases in which non-epistemic values 'conflict' with epistemic ones. For example, Resnik and Elliott (2019) consider a situation in which toxicologists have multiple options for how to design studies of a potentially toxic chemical and some study designs are more likely to uncover harmful effects of the chemical than other study designs. One might think that it would be questionable for the scientists to choose a study design that is relatively unlikely to turn up harmful effects, but it might not be entirely clear whether the choice of this design actually 'conflicts' with epistemic values.

Steel and Whyte (2012) argue that one can address many of the cases that worry Resnik and Elliott by appealing to a 'severity principle', according to which tests of hypotheses are epistemically acceptable only if, in cases where a hypothesis is false, the tests have the potential to generate results that run contrary to it. However, it is doubtful that this principle is sufficient to address all concerns about the values-in-science standard; problems can still arise even in cases where study designs are compatible with the severity principle and other epistemic standards. For example, Bennett Holman and Justin Bruner (2017) explore cases in which pharmaceutical companies preferentially fund researchers who employ study designs favourable to their products. Even if these study designs appeared to be acceptable, the evidence available to the scientific community and the conclusions drawn from that evidence could still be skewed in worrisome ways through preferential funding of this sort (see also Elliott and McKaughan 2009; Okruhlik 1994; Winsberg 2018, 137).

4.3 Preserving the Objectivity of the Scientific Community

Building on Holman and Bruner's observation that problems can arise not only through the actions of individual scientists but also through the structure of the scientific community, one might shift focus towards managing values at the level of the scientific community as a whole. For example, Helen Longino's approach to handling the implications of her gap argument was not to focus on particular kinds of values or roles for values but instead to focus on structuring the scientific community in such a way that value influences could be critically evaluated. She argued that the scientific community should be striving for objectivity, and she contended that objectivity is achieved not by eliminating values but by achieving critical reflection about them. She proposed four main criteria that one could employ to determine whether the community was structured appropriately for achieving critical reflection: the existence of publicly recognised venues for criticism, uptake of criticism, shared standards, and tempered equality of intellectual authority (Longino 1990, 2002). According to Longino, objectivity emerges at the level of the scientific community when these four criteria are met, thereby facilitating transformative criticism of background assumptions and the values associated with them. Miriam Solomon (2001) offers a similar account of scientific objectivity and the management of value judgements that focuses on the scientific community rather than on individual scientists. Rather than trying to eliminate or limit the role of non-epistemic values (which she calls 'decision vectors'), she argues that the influences of these values are acceptable when each of the theories or hypotheses under consideration by the scientific community is favoured by roughly the same number of non-epistemic values (or, as Solomon would put it, 'non-empirical decision vectors'; Solomon 2001, 77).

This shift to focusing on the scientific community as the locus of objectivity is extremely insightful, but it is not without its challenges. One worry is that these accounts do not put any in-principle constraints on the sorts of values or decision vectors that can be considered. So, for example, Intemann (2017) worries that some individual scientists could be allowed to incorporate highly racist or sexist values into their background assumptions on these accounts. Longino and Solomon would surely argue that if the scientific community were structured appropriately to achieve transformative criticism or to balance out these non-epistemic values, then these repugnant values would not have an undue influence on the community as a whole. Nevertheless, one might think that there is something problematic about allowing these sorts of values into scientific consideration rather than substantively excluding them as unacceptable.

Another worry is that it could be challenging to apply Longino's and Solomon's criteria in practice. For example, Inmaculada de Melo-Martín and Kristen Intemann (2018) have argued that it is difficult to distinguish appropriate and inappropriate forms of scientific dissent using Longino's criteria. Presumably, her criteria should be useful for identifying cases of inappropriate dissent, such as cases where interest groups manufacture doubt about tobacco smoking or evolutionary theory or climate change. However, de Melo-Martín and Intemann show that it can be surprisingly difficult in practice to determine whether Longino's criteria have actually been violated. For example, they point out that when sceptics are accused of failing to take up criticism of their views from other scientific perspectives, the sceptics can argue that they are in fact meaningfully engaging with their critics but that they are resisting the criticisms because they have adequate responses (de Melo-Martín and Intemann 2018, 47).

Similarly, in the case of Solomon's account, it is likely to be difficult to discern in practice whether non-empirical decision vectors (i.e., values) are equally distributed across different theories. First, there are so many different kinds of non-empirical factors that could affect scientists' reasoning that it is doubtful whether one could make a precise enough count of them to determine whether they were equally distributed. Second, some factors could influence scientists much more intensely than others, so it is not clear that a mere count of the values on each side of a controversy would provide an adequate indication of whether the scientific community was being unduly influenced by non-empirical factors.

4.4 Bringing Different Strategies Together

Given the difficulties associated with all these strategies for managing values in scientific reasoning, one might try to bring several of them together in a combined approach. I tried something along these lines in my book, *A Tapestry of Values* (Elliott 2017). I argued in favour of three conditions for responsibly managing values in science: (1) transparency, (2) representativeness, and (3) engagement. The first condition provides an avenue for respecting the perspectives of those who have differing views about how values should influence science. When scientists are open about their data, methods, and assumptions, it ideally allows others to recognise how values have influenced scientific work so they can decide how they want to respond to it (e.g., accepting it, rejecting it, or reinterpreting it). The second condition, representativeness, focuses on incorporating the right values in science, as discussed in Section 4.1; I contend that the values that influence science should be '*representative* of our major social and ethical priorities' (2017, 10, italics in original). My approach incorporates elements of both the ethical and the political approaches to identifying the right values. I argue that '[w]hen clear, widely recognized ethical principles are available, they should be used to guide the values that influence science' (2017, 14). However, given the complexity of arriving at shared ethical conclusions, I argue that '[w]hen ethical principles are less settled, science should be influenced as much as possible by values that represent broad societal priorities' (2017, 14–15). My third condition focuses on generating engagement between different scientists, community members, and scholars from a range of different fields. Engagement can be interpreted as an avenue for arriving at the 'right' values (e.g., by aligning the values of scientists with the values of the communities they aim to help), but it is also important for promoting the objectivity of the scientific community, as discussed in Section 4.3. As part of my account of engagement, I emphasise the importance of promoting diversity within the scientific community and generating communication between an interdisciplinary array of scholars in order to promote critical reflection on values in science.

Unfortunately, combined approaches have the potential to bring together not only the strengths but also the weaknesses of the individual strategies that they bring together. My goal in bringing together multiple approaches was to provide a more comprehensive framework that could make use of multiple criteria for distinguishing between legitimate and illegitimate influences of values. However, my combined approach still suffers from many of the weaknesses associated with the individual approaches on which I draw. For example, just as the approaches described in Sections 4.1 through 4.3 suffer from various ambiguities and differing ways of interpreting them, each of my three conditions (which draw to varying extents on these previous approaches) also suffer from a lack of specification.

Consider the condition of transparency. As I have emphasised in subsequent work (Elliott 2020b, 2021), transparency is an extremely complex concept. One needs to clarify what content needs to be communicated, what one aims to accomplish by providing the information, who should communicate it, who they should communicate it to, what venues to use for communicating it, and so on. Transparency can never be achieved perfectly, and it has costs as well as benefits (Elliott 2020b; John 2018; Quinn 2021), so it is important to specify more precisely how to achieve the kinds of transparency necessary for managing values appropriately.

My other conditions are similarly lacking. With respect to representativeness, I did not clarify the details of when to shift from an ethical approach to a political approach for identifying which values should influence scientific reasoning. Moreover, when pursuing a political approach, I did not specify how to figure out which values actually represent the views of a population. With respect to engagement, the crucial problem with my account is that very different results can emerge from an engagement effort depending on the rules of engagement and the participants in the effort (Kourany 2018). For example, a recent study that explored the implications of incorporating patients in health economics modelling highlighted a number of variables that could affect the outcomes of the process; these included the number of patients included, their identities, the power dynamics associated with the engagement effort, and the number and identity of other stakeholders who were also included (Harvard and Werker 2021). Without specifying these sorts of details, my account of engagement is incomplete.

Of course, the lack of detail about these three conditions is not a devastating problem; they can be specified and elaborated. A deeper worry is that they are neither necessary nor sufficient by themselves for managing values in science.

I have previously acknowledged that these conditions are more like rules of thumb rather than necessary and sufficient conditions for distinguishing legitimate and illegitimate roles for values in science (Elliott 2018), but one might want something more precise and complete than just my rules of thumb. For example, one of their major limitations is that they do not identify roles for values in science that are inherently problematic (see, e.g., the strategies discussed in Section 4.2). One might think that there are some ways of bringing values into scientific reasoning that are always unacceptable (e.g., falsifying data or designing studies in ways that do not provide severe tests of the hypotheses under investigation). Although I could probably reject these problematic activities in most cases based on my existing conditions, one might want to rule out these activities more explicitly (see, e.g., Steel 2017; Steel and Whyte 2012). Thus, my account arguably needs to be not only specified but also extended to include additional conditions.

5 What Are Some Next Steps?

Section 4 showed that the existing recommendations for managing values in science are imperfect. As a result, this is likely to be a vibrant area for future research. It remains to be seen what approach will ultimately be best, but in this section, I outline a path forward that builds on the mixed strategy in my previous book (Elliott 2017) and extends it to include additional insights from others who have been working on this problem. One of the important lessons to take from the previous approaches discussed throughout Section 4 is that it is very difficult to provide one or two conditions that are necessary and sufficient for managing values in science.[25] There are so many ways that values can relate to science, so many fields of science, and so many different contexts in which science is used that a realistic approach to handling values in science needs to incorporate multiple norms that can be adapted for different situations.[26]

Moreover, as Douglas (2018) has argued, these norms should apply not only to *individual scientists* but also to a range of *institutions*. For example, in order to manage values in science effectively, it might be necessary to provide guidance to journals, universities, scientific societies, funding agencies, and even media outlets. Moreover, given that the private sector now funds more than two-thirds of the scientific research and development occurring around the world (OECD 2021), it is important to explore norms for managing the activity of private companies. Although the private sector has undoubtedly produced

---

[25] I thank David Resnik for helping me to think through this point.

[26] I am using the term 'norms' rather than referring to 'conditions' or 'principles' in order to emphasise that these norms are often informal and not fully specified in terms of formal rules, principles, or necessary and sufficient conditions.

important scientific innovations that have served the public good (Holman and Elliott 2018), companies have also engaged in a wide range of problematic research activities that need to be constrained (see, e.g., McGarity and Wagner 2008; Michaels 2008; Oreskes and Conway 2010; Sismondo 2018). This section sketches out the general contours of a norm-based approach that can apply both to individuals and to institutions.

5.1 A Norm-Based Approach to Managing Values

I suggest that those seeking to manage values in science develop a set of multiple norms that are designed to prevent values from having inappropriate influences on science (see Table 5). On this account, values can appropriately influence science as long as scientists and scientific institutions follow the norms for good scientific practice. Building on the 'right values' approach (Section 4.1), one of these norms could be that science should be done in a way that serves the social good. Drawing from the 'roles for values' approach (Section 4.2), norms like honesty, accuracy, and reproducibility could be used to block scientists from accepting claims just because they fit their value preferences. Pulling from the 'objectivity and the scientific community' approach (Section 4.3), a norm like transformative criticism could be employed and specified using Longino's four criteria. Drawing from my mixed approach to managing values in science (Section 4.4), norms like transparency and engagement could also be added. Given that the concept of engagement in my previous book (Elliott 2017) incorporates both engagement with communities and the pursuit of diverse perspectives within the scientific community, it could be split into two norms: 'community engagement' and 'promotion of diversity, equity, and inclusion'. Additional norms, such as protection of human and animal research subjects, could be added to reflect scientists' responsibilities for

Table 5 A partial list of norms for good science (see also Resnik and Elliott 2019)

- Social good
- Honesty
- Accuracy
- Reproducibility
- Transformative criticism
- Transparency
- Community engagement
- Promotion of diversity, equity, and inclusion
- Protection of human and animal research subjects

handling values not only in 'doing science' but also in other categories like 'managing science' that were discussed in Section 2. One of the virtues of an approach like this is that one could keep adding other norms as gaps or limitations in the existing norms became apparent.

However, as critics pointed out in response to the three 'rules of thumb' I proposed in my earlier work, there are at least two worries associated with this kind of approach (see, e.g., Brown 2018; Douglas 2018; Kourany 2018). First, these norms are of limited use unless they are specified more precisely. As Section 4.4 emphasised, there are many details involved in promoting a norm like transparency or engagement, so ultimately the extent to which these norms protect science from inappropriate value influences depends on how these norms are interpreted and implemented. Second, in complex cases, these norms have the potential to conflict with each other, so one must decide how to prioritise them and manage these conflicts. For example, as Section 3 demonstrated when discussing the aims argument, the norm of accuracy and the norm of social good can come into conflict when regulatory agencies are trying to develop science that serves their practical purposes.

In my view, the best way to address these worries would be to combine these norms with two additional elements: a theoretical one and a practical one (see Figure 2). At a theoretical level, one could assess, evaluate, and justify these norms based on ethical and/or political analysis.[27] As Brown (2020) has emphasised, scientists need to engage in moral imagination to determine which norms are relevant and how they can best be implemented in specific contexts, given practical constraints and community concerns. They also frequently need to distinguish between the minimal behaviours that must be met in order to satisfy the norms, as compared with the ideal behaviours toward which they can be striving to the extent possible (Douglas 2014). Ethicists who specialise in analysing such issues could help to guide these decisions. In addition, political efforts of the sort Schroeder (2021) discusses

---

[27] It is worth noting that even though I am incorporating a 'theoretical' element in my account, my overall approach is still rather practically oriented, insofar as I start with a variety of scientific norms and then appeal to theoretical analysis primarily to help justify those norms and handle conflicts among them. Although I appeal to various theoretical approaches as a source of guidance, I am not particularly interested in debating which theoretical framework is best. In that sense, my approach is grounded in the norms that anchor scientific practice rather than the theories that explain or justify those practices. An alternative approach would be to start with a more substantive theoretical framework and use it as the starting point for developing a set of norms; my sense is that scholars like Brown (2020), Longino (1990, 2002), or Schroeder (2021, 2022) are more inclined to take such a theoretically based approach. Both approaches have strengths and weaknesses, but I am more comfortable taking a practically oriented approach. I thank Drew Schroeder for helping me think through the differences between more theoretically grounded versus more practically grounded ways to develop my norm-based approach.

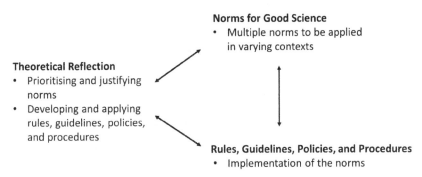

Figure 2 A representation of the relationships between theoretical reflection, norms, and their practical implementation in a norm-based approach to managing values in science

could also be used to help specify and prioritise norms in cases where there is sufficient time and interest. This theoretical analysis of the norms could also be informed by considering the aims of science and the ways those aims in particular contexts might call for different approaches to prioritising or applying the norms.

Admittedly, there are numerous details about this theoretical element of the account that would need to be worked out. For example, it would be important to consider when an ethical approach should be used as opposed to a political approach for prioritising and justifying the norms (see, e.g., Schroeder 2020). One might also wonder to what extent both approaches could be used together. It would also be important to decide whether particular aims for science were ethically or politically illegitimate and thus could not justifiably be used to defend norms for science. In light of these questions, it is best to view this proposal as a general outline or sketch to guide future work rather than as a fully formed account. One could fill in this sketch with different theoretical approaches to specifying the norms as well as different lists of norms.

In addition to the theoretical analysis of the norms, there would also need to be practical systems of rules, guidelines, policies, and procedures for implementing the norms (Table 6). This is an aspect of managing values in science that has been largely neglected by philosophers of science, but I suggest that it be part of future work on this topic. Most scientists do not have the time, energy, or inclination to think deeply about the range of value-laden judgements they face in their research. Thus, if value-laden judgements in science are to be handled appropriately, much of the thinking about how to handle them needs to be done in other settings and then passed on to scientists in the

Table 6 Examples of rules, guidelines, policies, and procedures for
implementing norms for good scientific practice (adapted with permission from
Resnik and Elliott 2019)[28]

- Policies and ethics codes related to social responsibility in research
- Policies that define and prohibit research misconduct, such as fabrication or falsification of data or plagiarism
- Rules or guidelines for designing experiments
- Rules or guidelines concerning standards of evidence for accepting or rejecting hypotheses
- Rules or guidelines concerning good statistical practice
- Policies and procedures for disclosing and describing materials and methods in publications and grant proposals
- Policies for disclosing and managing financial and other interests related to research
- Policies for sharing data, research materials (e.g., biological samples and chemical reagents), and computer codes
- Policies and procedures related to community engagement
- Rules, policies, and procedures prohibiting sexual harassment
- Rules, policies, and procedures pertaining to research with animal or human subjects

form of rules, guidelines, and lists of best practices. For example, journal editors often set policies about how data should be presented and shared, what kinds of statistical analyses should be used, and how results should be reported. A wide variety of other organisations, including scholarly societies, national academies of science, funding agencies, regulatory agencies, and universities, also create rules, codes, and guidelines to help ensure that norms of good science are followed.

As noted at the beginning of this section, however, it is important to direct rules and guidelines not only towards individual scientists but also towards private companies because these companies often face intense pressures to prioritise profits over the values that are most ethically or politically legitimate. In some cases, scientific journals can implement rules to encourage companies to follow norms for good science. For example, some medical journals now require public registration of clinical trial designs before studies are performed

---

[28] The rules and guidelines in Table 6 are listed in roughly the same order as the norms in Table 5 that these rules are designed to help implement. One could also organise them in terms of the scientific activities that they are designed to help regulate (e.g., steering science, doing science, using science, managing science), although some sets of rules (such as ethics codes related to socially responsible research) are likely to cut across many different scientific activities.

and independent statistical analysis of trial data by someone not involved in the study, as well as disclosures of the funding sources for clinical trials and/or disclosures of the roles that different authors played in the production of manuscripts (see, e.g., Sismondo 2018). Because private companies often do not publish their research, however, other entities, such as regulatory agencies, also have important roles to play in implementing guidelines for private companies. For example, after fraud was uncovered in privately funded toxicology studies during the 1970s, the US Food and Drug Administration created a set of Good Laboratory Practice guidelines to govern studies submitted for regulatory approval (Elliott 2016). Many commentators have argued that regulatory agencies should also require that the scientific data submitted to them by private companies be made publicly available so that the data can be scrutinised by outside experts (see, e.g., McGarity and Wagner 2008; Michaels 2008). It is also important to recognise that companies can be influenced to follow norms for good science using 'carrots' as well as 'sticks'. For example, patent policies, public–private partnerships, and government subsidies can all be used to incentivise some forms of research over others.

As shown in Figure 2, theoretical reflection is crucial for developing these rules and policies, critiquing them, and determining how to apply them in specific situations. It is important to promote critical reflection on these rules and policies because otherwise they can block scientific innovation and become overly restrictive, out of date, and ineffective (de Melo-Martín and Intemann 2018; Elliott 2016; Holman 2015).[29] Philosophers of science are well placed to help scientific organisations reflect on their rules and policies and to consider when deviations from accepted practices are warranted and how best to communicate transparently about those deviations (de Winter 2016).

It is important to emphasise that the theoretical reflection involved in prioritising norms and implementing rules could be enriched by studying how those norms and rules play out in actual scientific practice. This mutually informing relationship between theoretical reflection, application of norms, and implementation of rules is represented in Figure 2 with bidirectional arrows between the three elements of the figure. In this respect, the model proposed here has much in common with the notion of reflective equilibrium, which is commonly employed in practical ethics (see, e.g., Daniels 2016; Rawls 1971). The core idea of reflective equilibrium is that our ethical views can be justified by working back and forth to develop coherence between our considered moral judgements and the theoretical principles that govern those judgements. I do not go so far as to say that the three elements in Figure 2 are actually justified based

---

[29] I thank Robyn Bluhm for emphasising this point.

on their coherence with each other, but I do think that each element of the figure ought to be informed by the other elements.[30]

5.2 Illustrating the Approach

To see how the three elements of the approach represented in Figure 2 work together, consider the norm of transparency as an example. In science, the word 'transparency' is typically used as a metaphor to refer to openness about data, methods, conflicts of interest, and interpretive judgements (Elliott 2020b). There are multiple ways that one could justify this norm from a theoretical perspective. First, when scientists are open about their data and methods they enable others to scrutinise their work and potentially identify important value-laden judgements associated with it. Second, when scientists are open about their conflicts of interest, it can help warn other scientists of the possibility that the research could be influenced by values that merit further scrutiny (although it is important to acknowledge that this kind of disclosure might not always be as helpful as it initially appears; see de Melo-Martín and Intemann 2009; Elliott 2008). Third, when scientists are open about specific value-laden judgements associated with their work, it helps preserve the self-determination of the decision-makers who make use of it. Once decision-makers recognise that specific judgements have been made, they can reflect on whether they agree with those judgements and whether the resulting science is appropriate for their purposes. This is important in a pluralistic society because even if scientists have engaged in thoughtful ethical or political reflection about how best to handle the judgements associated with their work, there will typically be others who disagree with those choices.

Additional theoretical reflection is important for deciding how to apply a norm like transparency. Achieving openness about data, methods, and value judgements takes time, energy, and money, and it can also generate conflicts with other norms (Quinn 2021). Consider, for example, a major conflict that played out at the US Environmental Protection Agency (EPA) during the Trump administration. The EPA proposed a new 'Transparency Rule' that would allow the agency to disregard scientific studies if the data underlying those studies were not made sufficiently available for public scrutiny (Malakoff 2019). Despite its potential to promote transparency, many scientific societies, journals, and non-governmental organisations opposed the rule because it could have been used as an excuse to ignore or devalue important studies when they included confidential patient information that could not be released publicly.

---

[30] I am grateful to Kristen Intemann for helping me think through the relationships among the elements in this figure.

Thus, the debate over this rule illustrates how the norms of serving society and protecting human research subjects can conflict with the norm of transparency. Ultimately, the EPA received more than 600,000 public comments about how to handle this conflict, prominent scientists weighed in with reflections on its pros and cons, and environmental groups like the Environmental Defense Fund sued the agency to keep the rule from being implemented (Allison and Fineberg 2020; Eilperin 2021). There is still room for more philosophical debate about how best to navigate the tensions between these norms, but it is encouraging to see that civil society spontaneously generated a great deal of valuable reflection in this case.

Turning to the practical implementation of this norm, there are an array of guidelines that can help scientists pursue transparency in a responsible fashion. For example, as part of the emerging 'open science' movement (see, e.g., NAS 2018), a committee of scientists developed a set of 'Transparency and Openness Promotion' guidelines (Nosek et al. 2015). These guidelines help scientific journals set expectations for how their authors should handle issues like sharing materials, publishing data and methods, pre-registering their studies before performing them, and citing other people's data. There are also a number of guidelines to help scientists report their results in an open and meaningful fashion. For example, the Consolidated Standards of Reporting Trials (CONSORT) is an influential system of guidelines in the medical field for reporting randomised clinical trials (Schulz et al. 2010). It includes a twenty-five-item checklist and a flow diagram to help authors report their results as responsibly as possible. An example from a different field is the Criteria for Reporting and Evaluating Ecotoxicity Data (CRED), which was developed both to help risk assessors evaluate the quality of aquatic ecotoxicology studies and to help those performing the studies to report their results as carefully as possible (Moermond et al. 2016). CRED includes fifty reporting elements divided into six categories. Guidelines like these do not spare individual scientists from all responsibility for reflecting on how to engage in transparency. They still have to make decisions about whether to follow a formal reporting system, which system to use, and how closely to follow it. Nevertheless, some of the responsibilities for making decisions about how to engage in transparency can be shifted to the guideline designers, who are able to deliberate and gather additional input on how to handle these choices.

5.3 Moving Forward with the Norm-Based Approach

My proposed norm-based approach opens up a number of research opportunities for philosophers of science. As we have seen in the case of transparency, the norms listed in Table 5 require extensive efforts at theoretical analysis and practical implementation. For example, many debates about the role of values in scientific reasoning involve tensions between the norm of promoting social good and more 'traditional' scientific norms like accuracy and reproducibility (Douglas and Elliott 2022; Hudson 2021). For instance, as we saw in Section 3, some proponents of the value-free ideal have tried to suggest ways in which scientists could 'hedge' their claims so that they could remain faithful to their data and avoid drawing value-laden conclusions (e.g., Betz 2013, 2017). However, critics of the value-free ideal have argued that those hedging strategies could leave decision-makers confused, thereby detracting from the policymaking process (e.g., Elliott 2011b; Frank 2017). Faced with these tensions, some philosophers have argued that it is possible to fully satisfy ethical norms like concern for social good while simultaneously satisfying other scientific norms (e.g., Brown 2020; Kourany 2010). The approach sketched in this section does not provide a single, straightforward answer about how to handle these debates. Rather, it affirms that multiple norms are in play and that the key to addressing conflicts or tensions between the norms is to engage in theoretical analysis about how to manage them. The discussion throughout Sections 4 and 5 has shown that this theoretical analysis is unlikely to generate simple rules that specify how to handle every case of tension between the norms. While there may be some general rules of thumb that can address most cases, scientific practice is diverse enough that different approaches to navigating norms are likely to be justified in different situations.[31]

A good example of recent efforts to engage in theoretical analysis of scientific norms comes from those who have been analysing the phenomenon of scientific dissent (see, e.g., Biddle and Leuschner 2015; de Melo-Martín and Intemann 2018; Le Bihan and Amadi 2017; Leuschner and Fernández Pinto 2021; Miller 2021). As Longino (1990) emphasised, critical interaction is an important norm in science because scientific claims need to be scrutinised from multiple perspectives in order to promote objectivity. Nevertheless, the critical scrutiny of scientific claims can sometimes clash with norms of honesty and accuracy, as illustrated by recent disinformation campaigns in which interest groups have sought to cast doubt on the scientific evidence about topics like human-induced climate change, pesticides, pharmaceuticals, evolution, vaccine safety, and COVID-19 (see, e.g., McGarity and Wagner 2008; Michaels 2008; Oreskes and Conway 2010). In response to

---

[31] As Kristen Intemann has pointed out to me, the extent to which we might want clear necessary and sufficient conditions for distinguishing appropriate and inappropriate scientific practices depends on the context in which we are operating. If we are developing rules for scientific misconduct, where the consequences for engaging in misconduct are severe, then it is important to have very clear criteria for specifying what misconduct is. If we are instead developing ideals for good scientific practice, then precise necessary and sufficient conditions are probably neither necessary nor feasible.

these difficulties, philosophers have been proposing a variety of principles designed to distinguish appropriate forms of criticism or dissent from those that are inappropriate (see, e.g., Biddle and Leuschner 2015; Le Bihan and Amadi 2017; Miller 2021). Inmaculada de Melo-Martín and Kristen Intemann (2018) have considered a number of these principles and have concluded, in much the same way as this Element, that efforts to provide universal criteria run into problems. Nevertheless, the burgeoning philosophical scholarship on this issue can provide valuable guidance for analysing specific instances of dissent and determining whether values might be playing a problematic role.

Philosophers can also analyse the rules, guidelines, policies, and procedures through which scientific norms are implemented. For example, in a paper that examined the testing of genetically modified maize, Fern Wickson and Brian Wynne (2012) argued that the guidelines provided by European regulatory agencies for testing the safety of genetically modified crops are based on value-laden judgements that merit further scrutiny. Their analysis provides a model for philosophers interested in analysing the guidelines promulgated by regulatory agencies like the European Food Safety Authority or the US Food and Drug Administration (see also Stegenga 2017). When these agencies set standards for the ways studies should be designed in order to inform agency decision-making, they make crucial value-laden judgements that can have a major influence on society at large. For example, as proponents of the error argument emphasise, it is typically the case that some ways of designing regulatory studies increase the risk of generating false-positive conclusions about the hazards of a product, while other ways of designing the studies increase the risk of generating false-negative conclusions. This can create significant social conflicts when regulatory agencies declare products to be safe on the basis of their preferred studies, while studies that employ alternative study designs indicate that the products could be problematic (see, e.g., Myers et al. 2009). In addition to challenging particular guidelines directly, philosophers can also sometimes make an important contribution by evaluating the processes through which these guidelines were formulated. In many cases, they are developed using procedures that are difficult for most stakeholders to access and understand, which means that the kind of transformative criticism promoted by Longino is unlikely to occur (Elliott 2016).

In sum, the norm-based approach outlined here has a number of strengths as a starting point for future work on managing values in science. First, by focusing on a list of norms, the approach interfaces well with norm-based approaches that research ethicists have used for managing values in the other aspects of science discussed in Section 2, such as 'steering' or 'managing' science (see, e.g., Resnik 1998). Given the fact that value influences can 'bleed' from one area of science to another (e.g., from the choice of research projects to scientific reasoning), there are significant benefits to pursuing an approach for managing values that can be applied across many different areas of science. Second, by focusing on *multiple* norms, the account is flexible. It can incorporate norms associated with several of the different approaches for managing values that were discussed in Section 4. Moreover, new norms can be added when needed, and the norms can be prioritised and applied differently to address a variety of contexts. Third, the approach acknowledges that theoretical analysis is needed in order to justify the norms and apply them appropriately. Admittedly, deciding how best to provide this theoretical analysis is very difficult; it could involve various theoretical perspectives associated with the different approaches discussed in Section 4. Fortunately, because the proposal laid out in this section is only a sketch designed to guide future research, it can be developed in different ways depending on one's views about these issues. Fourth, this approach is practical because it works with the rules, guidelines, policies, and procedures that shape real-world scientific practice. This is an important lesson: if philosophers of science really want to shape the intersection between science and values, they need to engage with the nitty-gritty realities of scientific practice and the institutions surrounding that practice at a concrete level. Taking all these strengths into account, the norm-based approach appears to provide a promising framework for moving forward, even if it leaves a number of the details and challenges associated with previous approaches still to be worked out.

6 Conclusion

In this Element, we have seen that science is awash in values. As shown in Figure 1, values can intersect with research agendas, with scientific reasoning, with the ways research is used and applied, and with the behaviour of scientists as they perform research. Many different kinds of values play into all these activities. Some scholars have tried to distinguish these values into epistemic ones (which are necessary for truth or help attain truth) and those that are non-epistemic, but this distinction has been the subject of intense debate. There are also many ways in which the choices or judgements involved in scientific practice can be 'value-laden'. In some cases, researchers are consciously motivated by particular values, but it is also important to consider cases in which scientists do not consciously consider values but make underdetermined choices that have an impact on important values.

Although all the roles for values shown in Figure 1 are important, philosophers of science have been especially interested in the ways in which values relate to scientific reasoning. A central research question has been whether scientists should deliberately incorporate values into this aspect of their work. On one hand, excluding or minimising values (especially non-epistemic values) might help scientists achieve their goal of generating true or reliable information about the world, and it could also help protect the self-determination and trust of those who depend on scientific information. On the other hand, Section 3 described four arguments (focusing on gaps, errors, aims, and concepts) for deliberately incorporating non-epistemic values into scientific reasoning. Subsequent debates about the strengths and weaknesses of these arguments suggest that there are at least some cases in which non-epistemic values should play a deliberate role in scientific reasoning. Some of the most compelling cases are those in which decision-makers need scientific guidance, value-laden judgements are unavoidable in the course of providing that guidance, and it would be unworkable for scientists to defer all those judgements to the decision-makers. Given the pervasive judgements that enter into scientific research, non-epistemic values arguably have important roles to play in many areas of science, but the details of these roles continue to be a matter of debate.

One of the most important issues that merits further discussion is the question of how to manage the influences of values so they do not detract from the quality of scientific reasoning. Section 4 described a number of different proposals, including efforts to incorporate the 'right' values, attempts to limit the 'roles' that values play, and efforts to generate a critical assessment of values by the scientific community. Section 5 then sketched out a potential path for future research that incorporates elements from multiple previous proposals. This approach relies on a set of norms that are justified and prioritised based on theoretical analysis and implemented through a system of rules, guidelines, policies, and procedures. According to this view, the influences of values on scientific reasoning are appropriate as long as scientists and scientific institutions are following at least the minimum expectations of all the norms for good scientific practice (Douglas 2014). Perhaps the greatest weakness of this approach is that it is more of an outline for future research rather than a full-fledged account, so it raises unanswered questions about how to prioritise and implement norms when they come into conflict. Nevertheless, this approach also has major strengths, including the way it turns philosophers' attention towards the context-dependent nature of scientific norms and the importance of developing rules and guidelines for implementing them.

Section 5 showed that there are exciting opportunities for philosophers to become more engaged with the details of scientific practice and the institutions that guide scientific practice as they examine scientific norms and their implementation. This turn towards more engaged scholarship is currently a topic of significant interest in the field (Cartieri and Potochnik 2014; Fehr and Plaisance 2010; Plaisance and Elliott 2021), and philosophers can do engaged work that helps manage all four ways in which values intersect with science (see Figure 1). For example, Janet Kourany has been scrutinising the norms involved in *steering* science and arguing that sexist and racist values have skewed these norms in problematic ways (see, e.g., Kourany 2010, 2020). Kristin Shrader-Frechette has been scrutinising the norms involved in *doing* science and arguing that many environmental risk assessments rest on questionable models and interpretive judgements that serve polluters over affected communities (see, e.g., Shrader-Frechette 2014). Adam Briggle has been scrutinising the norms involved in *using* science and has argued that the regulation of hydraulic fracturing similarly serves the interests of polluters over affected communities (see, e.g., Briggle 2015). David Resnik has been scrutinising the norms involved in *managing* science and exploring how best to apply them to a wide array of research-ethics issues (e.g., Resnik 1998, 2007; Resnik et al. 2015).

These are just a few examples that illustrate a growing body of engaged scholarship. Philosophers are questioning the quality of the clinical trials and regulatory policies used for evaluating new medical interventions (Stegenga 2017, 2018), collaborating on projects with neuroscientists to explore the ethical implications of their research choices (Goering and Klein 2020a, 2020b), reflecting on how best to communicate information about public-health interventions and sensational scientific topics (Goldenberg 2021; Havstad 2021; Intemann 2020), examining whether the climate on science teams discourages the participation of under-represented minorities in science (Cech et al. 2021; Settles et al. 2019), critiquing the concepts and categories used in public health research and practice (Valles 2018; Katikireddi and Valles 2015), and working with Indigenous communities to develop plans for responding to climate change (Whyte et al. 2014). The philosophy-of-science community clearly has exciting opportunities to combine deep theoretical reflection with engaged, practical scholarship in an effort to promote a scientific research enterprise that is grounded in our deepest values.

References

Alexandrova, A. 2018. 'Can the Science of Well-Being be Objective?'. *British Journal for the Philosophy of Science* 69: 421–45.

Allison, D. and Fineberg, H. 2020. 'EPA's Proposed Transparency Rule: Factors to Consider, Many; Planets to Live on, One'. *Proceedings of the National Academy of Sciences* 117: 5084–7.

Anderson, E. 2004. 'Uses of Value Judgments in Science: A General Argument, with Lessons from a Case Study of Feminist Research on Divorce'. *Hypatia* 19: 1–24.

Barras, V. and Greub, G. 2014. 'History of Biological Warfare and Bioterrorism'. *Clinical Microbiology and Infection* 20: 497–502.

Betz, G. 2013. 'In Defence of the Value Free Ideal'. *European Journal for Philosophy of Science* 3: 207–20.

Betz, G. 2017. 'Why the Argument from Inductive Risk Doesn't Justify Incorporating Non-Epistemic Values in Scientific Reasoning'. In K. Elliott and D. Steel (eds.), *Current Controversies in Values and Science*, 94–110. London: Routledge.

Biddle, J. 2013. 'State of the Field: Transient Underdetermination and Values in Science'. *Studies in History and Philosophy of Science* 44: 124–33.

Biddle, J. and Kukla, R. 2017. 'The Geography of Epistemic Risk'. In K. Elliott and T. Richards (eds.), *Exploring Inductive Risk: Case Studies of Values in Science*, 215–38. New York: Oxford University Press.

Biddle, J. and Leuschner, A. 2015. 'Climate Skepticism and the Manufacture of Doubt: Can Dissent in Science be Epistemically Detrimental?'. *European Journal for Philosophy of Science* 5: 261–78.

Biddle, J. and Winsberg, E. 2010. 'Value Judgments and the Estimation of Uncertainty in Climate Modeling'. In P. D. Magnus and J. Busch (eds.), *New Waves in Philosophy of Science*, 172–97. New York: Palgrave Macmillan.

Bluhm, R. 2017. 'Inductive Risk and the Role of Values in Clinical Trials'. In K. Elliott and T. Richards (eds.), *Exploring Inductive Risk: Case Studies of Values in Science*, 193–212. New York: Oxford University Press.

Boulicault, M. and Schroeder, A. 2021. 'Public Trust in Science: Exploring the Idiosyncrasy-Free Ideal'. In K. Vallier and M. Weber (eds.), *Social Trust: Foundational and Philosophical Issues*, 102–21. New York: Routledge.

Brigandt, I. 2020. 'How to Philosophically Tackle Kinds without Talking About "Natural Kinds"'. *Canadian Journal of Philosophy*: 1–24. http://doi.org/10.1017/can.2029.20

Briggle, A. 2015. *A Field Philosopher's Guide to Fracking: How One Texas Town Stood Up to Big Oil and Gas*. New York: Liveright.

Bright, L. K. 2018. 'Du Bois' Democratic Defence of the Value Free Ideal'. *Synthese* 195: 2227–45.

Bronen, R. and Cochran, P. 2021. 'Decolonize Climate Adaptation Research'. *Science* 372: 1245.

Brown, M. 2018. 'Weaving Value Judgment into the Tapestry of Science'. *Philosophy, Theory, and Practice in Biology* 10: 8. http://doi.org/10.3998 /ptpbio.16039257.0010.010

Brown, M. 2020. *Science and Moral Imagination: A New Ideal for Values in Science*. Pittsburgh: University of Pittsburgh Press.

Cartieri, F. and Potochnik, A. 2014. 'Toward Philosophy of Science's Social Engagement'. *Erkenntnis* 79: 901–16.

Cech, E., Settles, I. H., Cheruvelil, K. S. et al. 2021. 'The Social is Professional: The Effects of Team Climate on Professional Outcomes for LGBTQ Persons in Environmental Science'. *Journal of Women and Minorities in Science and Engineering* 27: 25–48.

Chastain, D. B., Osae, S. P., Henao-Martínez, A. F. et al. 2020. 'Racial Disproportionality in Covid Clinical Trials'. *New England Journal of Medicine*, 383(9): e59.

Cho, M. 2006. 'Racial and Ethnic Categories in Biomedical Research: There Is No Baby in the Bathwater'. *Journal of Law, Medicine & Ethics* 34: 497–9.

ChoGlueck, C. 2018. 'The Error Is in the Gap: Synthesizing Accounts for Societal Values in Science'. *Philosophy of Science* 85: 704–25.

Claudio, L. 2000. 'Reaching Out to New York Neighborhoods'. *Environmental Health Perspectives* 108: A450–A451.

Clough, S. and Loges, W. 2008. 'Racist Value Judgements as Objectively False Beliefs: A Philosophical and Social-Psychological Analysis'. *Journal of Social Philosophy* 39: 77–95.

Cornwall, W. 2020. 'Should Researchers Shelve Plans to Deliberately Infect People with the Coronavirus?'. *Science* (20 November). doi: 10.1126/science.abf8131

Daniels, N. 2016. 'Reflective Equilibrium'. *Stanford Encyclopedia of Philosophy*. https://plato.stanford.edu/entries/reflective-equilibrium/

de Melo-Martín, I. and Intemann, K. 2009. 'How Do Disclosure Policies Fail? Let Us Count the Ways'. *The FASEB Journal* 23: 1638–42.

de Melo-Martín, I. and Intemann, K. 2016. 'The Risk of Using Inductive Risk to Challenge the Value-Free Ideal'. *Philosophy of Science* 83: 500–520.

de Melo-Martín, I. and Intemann, K. 2018. *The Fight against Doubt: How to Bridge the Gap between Scientists and the Public*. New York: Oxford University Press.

de Vos, A. 2020. 'The Problem of "Colonial Science"'. *Scientific American*. (1 July).www.scientificamerican.com/article/the-problem-of-colonial-science/

de Winter, J. 2016. *Interests and Epistemic Integrity in Science: A Framework to Assess Interest Influences in Scientific Research Processes*. Lanham: Lexington Books.

DeVito, S. C. 2016. 'On the Design of Safer Chemicals: A Path Forward'. *Green Chemistry* 18: 4332–47.

DiMarco, M. and Khalifa, K. 2019. 'Inquiry Tickets: Values, Pursuit, and Underdetermination'. *Philosophy of Science* 86: 1016–28.

Douglas, H. 2000. 'Inductive Risk and Values in Science'. *Philosophy of Science* 67: 559–79.

Douglas, H. 2008. 'The Role of Values in Expert Reasoning'. *Public Affairs Quarterly* 22: 1–18.

Douglas, H. 2009. *Science, Policy, and the Value-Free Ideal*. Pittsburgh: University of Pittsburgh Press.

Douglas, H. 2013. 'The Value of Cognitive Values'. *Philosophy of Science* 80: 796–806.

Douglas, H. 2014. 'The Moral Terrain of Science'. *Erkenntnis* 79: 961-979.

Douglas, H. 2016. 'Values in Science'. In P. Humphreys (ed.), *The Oxford Handbook of Philosophy of Science*, 609–32. New York: Oxford University Press.

Douglas, H. 2017. 'Why Inductive Risk Requires Values in Science'. In K. Elliott and D. Steel (eds.), *Current Controversies in Values and Science*, 81–93. New York: Routledge.

Douglas, H. 2018. 'From Tapestry to Loom: Broadening the Perspective on Values in Science'. *Philosophy, Theory, and Practice in Biology* 10: 8. http://doi.org/10.3998/ptpbio.16039257.0010.008

Douglas, H. 2021. *The Rightful Place of Science: Science, Values, and Democracy. The 2016 Descartes Lectures*, ed. T. Richards. Tempe: Consortium for Science, Policy, and Outcomes.

Douglas, H. and Elliott, K. 2022. 'Addressing the Reproducibility Crisis: A Response to Hudson'. *Journal of General Philosophy of Science*. https://doi.org/10.1007/s10838-022-09606-5

Dupré, J. 2007. 'Fact and Value'. In H. Kincaid, A. Wylie, and J. Dupré (eds.), *Value-Free Science? Ideals and Illusions*, 27–41. New York: Oxford University Press.

Eilperin, J. 2021. 'Judge Throws Out Trump Rule Limiting What Science EPA Can Use'. *Washington Post* (1 February). www.washingtonpost.com/climate-environment/2021/02/01/trump-secret-science/

Elliott, K. 2008. 'Scientific Judgment and the Limits of Conflict-of-Interest Policies'. *Accountability in Research: Policies and Quality Assurance* 15: 1–29.

Elliott, K. 2009. 'The Ethical Significance of Language in the Environmental Sciences: Case Studies from Pollution Research'. *Ethics, Place & Environment* 12: 157–73.

Elliott, K. 2011a. 'Direct and Indirect Roles for Values in Science'. *Philosophy of Science* 78: 303–24.

Elliott, K. 2011b. *Is a Little Pollution Good for You? Incorporating Societal Values in Environmental Research*. New York: Oxford University Press.

Elliott, K. 2013. 'Douglas on Values: From Indirect Roles to Multiple Goals'. *Studies in History and Philosophy of Science* 44: 375–83.

Elliott, K. 2016. 'Standardized Study Designs, Value Judgments, and Financial Conflicts of Interest in Research'. *Perspectives on Science* 24: 529–51.

Elliott, K. 2017. *A Tapestry of Values: An Introduction to Values in Science*. New York: Oxford University Press.

Elliott, K. 2018. 'A Tapestry of Values: Response to My Critics'. *Philosophy, Theory, and Practice in Biology* 10 (11).

Elliott, K. 2020a. 'Framing Conservation: "Biodiversity" and the Values Embedded in Scientific Language'. *Environmental Conservation* 47: 260–8.

Elliott, K. 2020b. 'A Taxonomy of Transparency in Science'. *Canadian Journal of Philosophy*. http://doi.org/10.1017/can.2020.21

Elliott, K. 2021. 'The Value-Ladenness of Transparency in Science: Lessons from Lyme Disease'. *Studies in History and Philosophy of Science* 88: 1–9.

Elliott, K., McCright, A. M., Allen, S. and Dietz, T. 2017. 'Values in Environmental Research: Citizens' Views of Scientists Who Acknowledge Values'. *PloS One* 12: e0186049.

Elliott, K. and McKaughan, D. J. 2009. 'How Values in Scientific Discovery and Pursuit Alter Theory Appraisal'. *Philosophy of Science* 76: 598–611.

Elliott, K. and McKaughan, D. J. 2014. 'Nonepistemic Values and the Multiple Goals of Science'. *Philosophy of Science* 81: 1–21.

Elliott, K. and Resnik, D. B. 2014. 'Science, Policy, and the Transparency of Values'. *Environmental Health Perspectives* 122: 647–50.

Elliott, K. and Resnik, D. B. 2019. 'Making Open Science Work for Science and Society'. *Environmental Health Perspectives* 127: 075002.

Elliott, K. and Richards, T. 2017a. *Exploring Inductive Risk: Case Studies of Values in Science*. New York: Oxford University Press.

Elliott, K. and Richards, T. 2017b. 'Exploring Inductive Risk: Future Questions'. In K. C. Elliott and T. Richards (eds.), *Exploring Inductive*

Risk: Case Studies of Values in Science, 261–77. New York: Oxford University Press.

Elliott, K. and Willmes, D. 2013. 'Cognitive Attitudes and Values in Science'. *Philosophy of Science* 80, 807–17.

Fehr, C. and Plaisance, K. S. 2010. 'Socially Relevant Philosophy of Science: An Introduction'. *Synthese* 177: 301–16.

Fernández Pinto, M. and Hicks, D. J. 2019. 'Legitimizing Values in Regulatory Science'. *Environmental Health Perspectives* 127: 035001.

Franco, P. 2017. 'Assertion, Non-Epistemic Values, and Scientific Practice'. *Philosophy of Science* 84: 160–80.

Frank, D. 2017. 'Making Uncertainties Explicit: The Jeffreyan Value-Free Ideal and Its Limits'. In K. Elliott and T. Richards (eds.), *Exploring Inductive Risk: Case Studies of Values in Science*, 79–100. New York: Oxford University Press.

Frodeman, R., Klein, J. and Dos Santos Pache, R.co, eds. 2017. *The Oxford Handbook of Interdisciplinarity*. Oxford: Oxford University Press.

Goering, S. and Klein, E. 2020a. 'Embedding Ethics in Neural Engineering: An Integrated Transdisciplinary Collaboration'. In E. Brister and R. Frodeman (eds.), *A Guide to Field Philosophy: Case Studies and Practical Strategies*, 17–34. New York: Routledge.

Goering, S. and Klein, E. 2020b. 'Fostering Neuroethics Integration with Neuroscience in the BRAIN Initiative: Comments on the NIH Neuroethics Roadmap'. *AJOB Neuroscience* 11: 184–8.

Goldenberg, M. J. 2021. *Vaccine Hesitancy: Public Trust, Expertise, and the War on Science*. Pittsburgh: University of Pittsburgh Press.

Harris, R. 2017. *Rigor Mortis: How Sloppy Science Creates Worthless Cures, Crushes Hope, and Wastes Billions*. New York: Basic Books.

Harvard, S. and Werker, G. 2021. 'Health Economists on Involving Patients in Modeling: Potential Benefits, Harms, and Variables of Interest'. *PharmacoEconomics* 39: 823–33.

Harvard, S. and Winsberg, E. 2021. 'The Epistemic Risk in Representation'. *Kennedy Institute of Ethics Journal* 32: 1–31.

Havstad, J. 2021. 'Sensational Science, Archaic Hominin Genetics, and Amplified Inductive Risk'. *Canadian Journal of Philosophy*. http://doi.org /10.1017/can.2021.15

Havstad, J. and Brown, M. 2017. 'Inductive Risk, Deferred Decisions, and Climate Science Advising'. In K. Elliott and T. Richards (eds.), *Exploring Inductive Risk: Case Studies of Values in Science*, 101–23. New York: Oxford University Press.

Hicks, D. 2014. 'A New Direction for Science and Values'. *Synthese* 191: 3271–95.

Hilgartner, S., Hurlbut, J. B. and Jasanoff, S. 2021. 'Was "Science" on the Ballot?'. *Science* 371: 893–4.

Holman, B. H. 2015. *The Fundamental Antagonism: Science and Commerce in Medical Epistemology*. PhD Dissertation, University of California, Irvine.

Holman, B. and Bruner, J. 2017. 'Experimentation by Industrial Selection'. *Philosophy of Science* 84: 1008–19.

Holman, B. and Elliott, K. C. 2018. 'The Promise and Perils of Industry-Funded Science'. *Philosophy Compass* 13: e12544.

Holman, B. and Wilholt, T. 2022. 'The New Demarcation Problem'. *Studies in History and Philosophy of Science* 91: 211–20.

Howard, D. 2009. 'Better Red Than Dead – Putting an End to the Social Irrelevance of Postwar Philosophy of Science'. *Science and Education* 18: 199–220.

Hudson, R. 2021. 'Should We Strive to Make Science Bias-Free? A Philosophical Assessment of the Reproducibility Crisis'. *Journal for General Philosophy of Science* 52: 389–405.

Iacobucci, G. 2021. 'Covid-19: How Will a Waiver on Vaccine Patents Affect Global Supply?'. *British Medical Journal* 373. http://doi.org/10.1136/bmj .n1182

Intemann, K. 2005. 'Feminism, Underdetermination, and Values in Science'. *Philosophy of Science* 72: 1001–12.

Intemann, K. 2015. 'Distinguishing between Legitimate and Illegitimate Values in Climate Modeling'. *European Journal for Philosophy of Science* 5: 217–32.

Intemann, K. 2017. 'Feminism, Values, and the Bias Paradox'. In K. Elliott and D. Steel (eds.), *Current Controversies in Values and Science*, 130–44. New York: Routledge.

Intemann, K. 2020. 'Understanding the Problem of "Hype": Exaggeration, Values, and Trust in Science'. *Canadian Journal of Philosophy*: 1–16. http://doi.org/10.1017/can.2020.45

Jeffrey, R. 1956. 'Valuation and Acceptance of Scientific Hypotheses'. *Philosophy of Science* 23: 237–46.

Jenco, M. 2020. 'AAP: Include Children in COVID-19 Trials'. *AAP News* (17 November). www.aappublications.org/news/2020/11/17/covidvaccinetrials 111720

John, S. 2015a. 'The Example of the IPCC Does Not Vindicate the Value Free Ideal: A Response to Gregor Betz'. *European Journal for Philosophy of Science* 5: 1–13.

John, S. 2015b. 'Inductive Risk and the Contexts of Communication'. *Synthese* 192: 79–96.

John, S. 2018. 'Epistemic Trust and the Ethics of Science Communication: Against Transparency, Openness, Sincerity and Honesty'. *Social Epistemology* 32: 75–87.

John, S. 2019. 'Science, Truth, and Dictatorship: Wishful Thinking or Wishful Speaking?'. *Studies in History and Philosophy of Science* 78: 64–72.

Johnson, C., Kastanis, A. and Stafford, K. 2021. 'AP Analysis: Racial Disparity Seen in U.S. Vaccination Drive'. *AP News* (30 January). https://apnews.com/article/race-and-ethnicity-health-coronavirus-pandemic-hispanics-d0746b028cf56231dbcdeda0fba24314

Katikireddi, S. V. and Valles, S. A. 2015. 'Coupled Ethical–Epistemic Analysis of Public Health Research and Practice: Categorizing Variables to Improve Population Health and Equity'. *American Journal of Public Health* 105: e36–e42.

Kavanagh, E., ed. 2007. 'The Risks and Advantages of Framing Science'. *Science* 317: 1168–69.

Keller, E. F. and Longino, H., eds. 1996. *Feminism and Science*. New York: Oxford University Press.

Kendi, I. 2016. *Stamped from the Beginning: The Definitive History of Racist Ideas in America*. New York: Bold Type Books.

Kincaid, H., Dupré, J. and Wylie, A., eds. 2007. *Value-Free Science: Ideals and Illusions?* New York: Oxford University Press.

Kitcher, P. 2001. *Science, Truth, and Democracy*. New York: Oxford University Press.

Konings, F., Perkins, M. D., Kuhn, J. H. et al. 2021. 'SARS-CoV-2 Variants of Interest and Concern Naming Scheme Conducive for Global Discourse'. *Nature Microbiology* 6: 821–23

Korf, R. 2022. 'Can Democratic Processes Yield Democratic Values? The Influence of Science on Social Values'. Unpublished paper delivered at the Values in Science and Political Philosophy conference, Claremont, CA, 1 April.

Kourany, J. A. 2010. *Philosophy of Science after Feminism*. New York: Oxford University Press.

Kourany, J. A. 2013. 'Meeting the Challenges to Socially Responsible Science: Reply to Brown, Lacey, and Potter'. *Philosophical Studies* 163: 93–103.

Kourany, J. A. 2018. 'Adding to the Tapestry'. *Philosophy, Theory, and Practice in Biology* 10: 9. http://doi.org/10.3998/ptpbio.16039257.0010.009

Kourany, J. A. 2020. 'The New Worries about Science'. *Canadian Journal of Philosophy*: 1–19. http://doi.org/10.1017/can.2020.34

Kreber, C. 2009. *The University and its Disciplines: Teaching and Learning within and beyond Disciplinary Boundaries*. New York: Routledge.

Kuhn, T. 1977. 'Objectivity, Value Judgement, and Theory Choice'. In T. Kuhn (ed.), *The Essential Tension*, 320–9. Chicago: University of Chicago Press.

Lacey, H. 1999. *Is Science Value Free? Values and Scientific Understanding.* New York: Routledge.

Lacey, H. 2017. 'Distinguishing between Cognitive and Social Values'. In K. Elliott and D. Steel (eds.), *Current Controversies in Values and Science*, 15–30. New York: Routledge.

Larson, B. 2011. *Metaphors for Environmental Sustainability: Redefining Our Relationships with Nature.* New Haven: Yale University Press.

Le Bihan, S. and Amadi, I. 2017. 'On Epistemically Detrimental Dissent: Contingent Enabling Factors versus Stable Difference-Makers'. *Philosophy of Science* 84: 1020–30.

Leuschner, A. and Fernández Pinto, M. 2021. 'How Dissent on Gender Bias in Academia Affects Science and Society: Learning from the Case of Climate Change Denial'. *Philosophy of Science* 88: 573–93.http://doi.org/10.1086/713903

Levi, I. 1960. 'Must the Scientist Make Value Judgements?'. *Journal of Philosophy* 57: 345–57.

Longino, H. 1990. *Science as Social Knowledge.* Princeton: Princeton University Press.

Longino, H. 1996. 'Cognitive and Non-Cognitive Values in Science: Rethinking the Dichotomy'. In L. Hankinson Nelson and J. Nelson (eds.), *Feminism, Science, and the Philosophy of Science*, 39–58. Boston: Kluwer.

Longino, H. 2002. *The Fate of* Knowledge. Princeton: Princeton University Press.

Ludwig, D. 2016. 'Ontological Choices and the Value-Free Ideal'. *Erkenntnis* 81: 1253–72.

Lusk, G. 2020. 'Political Legitimacy in the Democratic View: The Case of Climate Services'. *Philosophy of Science* 87: 991–1002.

Machamer, P. and Wolters, G. 2004. *Science, Values, and Objectivity.* Pittsburgh: University of Pittsburgh Press.

Malakoff, D. 2019. '"Secret Science" Plan is Back, and Critics Say It's Worse'. *Science* 366: 783–4.

McGarity, T. and Wagner, W. 2008. *Bending Science: How Special Interests Corrupt Public Health Research.* Cambridge, MA: Harvard University Press.

McKaughan, D. and Elliott, K. C. 2015. 'Introduction: Cognitive Attitudes and Values in Science'. *Studies in History and Philosophy of Science* 53: 57–61.

McMullin, E. 1983. 'Values in Science'. In P. Asquith and T. Nickles (eds.), *PSA 1982*, 3–28. East Lansing: Philosophy of Science Association.

Mervis, J. and Kaiser, J. 2018. 'NSF Issues Sexual Harassment Policy as NIH Promises Action'. *Science* 361: 6409–10.

Michaels, D. 2008. *Doubt Is Their Product: How Industry's Assault on Science Threatens Your Health*. New York: Oxford University Press.

Miller, B. 2021. 'When Is Scientific Dissent Epistemically Inappropriate?'. *Philosophy of Science* 88: 918–28.

Moermond, C. T., Kase, R., Korkaric, M. and Ågerstrand, M. 2016. 'CRED: Criteria for Reporting and Evaluating Ecotoxicity Data'. *Environmental Toxicology and Chemistry* 35: 1297–1309.

Myers, J. P., vom Saal, F. S., Akingbemi, B. T. et al. 2009. 'Why Public Health Agencies Cannot Depend on Good Laboratory Practices as a Criterion for Selecting Data: The Case of Bisphenol A'. *Environmental Health Perspectives* 117: 309–15.

National Academies of Sciences, Engineering, and Medicine (NAS). 2018. *Open Science by Design: Realizing a Vision for 21st Century Research*. Washington, DC: The National Academies Press.

Nelson, L. H. 1990. *Who Knows: From Quine to a Feminist Epistemology*. Philadelphia: Temple University Press.

Nisbet, M. and Mooney, C. 2007. 'Science and Society. Framing Science'. *Science* 316: 56.

Norton, J. 2021. 'The Material Theory of Induction'. www.pitt.edu/~jdnorton/papers/material_theory/Material_Induction_March_14_2021.pdf

Nosek, B. A., Alter, G., Banks, G. C. et al. 2015. 'Promoting an Open Research Culture'. *Science* 348: 1422–5.

OECD. 2021. *OECD Science, Technology and Innovation Outlook 2021: Times of Crisis and Opportunity*. Paris: OECD. http://doi.org/10.1787/75f79015-en

Okruhlik, K. 1994. 'Gender and the Biological Sciences'. *Canadian Journal of Philosophy* 20(Supplementary): 21–42.

Oreskes, N. and Conway, E. 2010. *Merchants of Doubt: How a Handful of Scientists Obscured the Truth on Issues from Tobacco Smoke to Global Warming*. New York: Bloomsbury.

Parker, W. and Lusk, G. 2019. 'Incorporating User Values into Climate Services'. *Bulletin of the American Meteorological Society* 100: 1643–50.

Pease, R. 2021. 'Accusations of Colonial Science Fly after Eruption'. *Science* 372: 1248–9.

Plaisance, K. and Elliott, K. 2021. 'A Framework for Analyzing Broadly Engaged Philosophy of Science'. *Philosophy of Science* 88: 594–615.

Plutynski, A. 2018. *Explaining Cancer: Finding Order in Disorder*. New York: Oxford University Press.

Polanyi, M. 1962. 'The Republic of Science'. *Minerva* 1: 54–73.

Quinn, A. 2021. 'Transparency and Secrecy in Citizen Science: Lessons from Herping'. *Studies in History and Philosophy of Science* 85: 208–17.

Rawls, J. 1971. *A Theory of Justice*. Cambridge, MA: Harvard University Press.

Resnik, D. B. 1998. *The Ethics of Science: An Introduction*. New York: Routledge.

Resnik, D. B. 2007. *The Price of Truth: How Money Affects the Norms of Science*. New York: Oxford University Press.

Resnik, D. B. and Elliott, K. C. 2019. 'Value-Entanglement and the Integrity of Scientific Research'. *Studies in History and Philosophy of Science* 75: 1–11.

Resnik, D. B., Elliott, K. C. and Miller, A. 2015. 'A Framework for Addressing Ethical Issues in Citizen Science'. *Environmental Science & Policy* 54: 475–81.

Reverby, S., ed. 2000. *Tuskegee's Truths: Rethinking the Tuskegee Syphilis Study*. Durham: University of North Carolina Press.

Rolin, K. 2015. 'Values in Science: The Case of Scientific Collaboration'. *Philosophy of Science* 82: 157–77.

Rooney, P. 1992. 'On Values in Science: Is the Epistemic/Non-epistemic Distinction Useful?' in D. Hull, M. Forbes, and K. Okruhlik (eds.), *Proceedings of the 1992 Biennial Meeting of the Philosophy of Science Association*, vol. 1, p. 13–22. East Lansing, MI: Philosophy of Science Association.

Rooney, P. 2017. 'The Borderlands between Epistemic and Non-Epistemic Values'. In K. Elliott and D. Steel (eds.), *Current Controversies in Values and Science*, 31–45. New York: Routledge.

Rudner, R. 1953. 'The Scientist Qua Scientist Makes Value Judgements'. *Philosophy of Science* 20: 1–6.

Schienke, E. W., Baum, S.D., Tuana, N., Davis, K.J., and Keller, K. 2011. 'Intrinsic Ethics Regarding Integrated Assessment Models for Climate Management'. *Science and Engineering Ethics* 17: 503–23.

Schroeder, S. A. 2017. 'Using Democratic Values in Science: An Objection and (Partial) Response'. *Philosophy of Science* 84: 1044–54.

Schroeder, S. A. 2019. 'Which Values Should Be Built into Economic Measures?'. *Economics and Philosophy* 35: 521–36.

Schroeder, S. A. 2020. 'Thinking about Values in Science: Ethical vs. Political Approaches'. *Canadian Journal of Philosophy*. http://doi.org/10.1017/can .2020.41

Schroeder, S. A. 2021. 'Democratic Values: A Better Foundation for Public Trust in Science'. *British Journal for the Philosophy of Science* 72:511–43. http://doi.org/10.1093/bjps/axz023

Schroeder, S. A. 2022. 'An Ethical Framework for Presenting Scientific Results to Policy-Makers'. *Kennedy Institute of Ethics Journal* 32: 33–67.

Schulz, K. F., Altman, D. G. and Moher, D. 2010. 'CONSORT 2010 Statement: Updated Guidelines for Reporting Parallel Group Randomised Trials'. *Trials* 11(1): 1–8.

Schwartz, S. and Bilsky, W. 1987. 'Toward a Universal Psychological Structure of Human Values'. *Journal of Personality and Social Psychology* 53: 550–62.

Scriven, M. 1974. 'The Exact Role of Value Judgements in Science'. In K. Schaffner and R. Cohen (eds.), *PSA 1972*, 219–47. Dordrecht: Reidel.

Settles, I. H., Brassel, S. T., Montgomery, G. M. et al. 2018. 'Missing the Mark: A New Form of Honorary Authorship Motivated by Desires for Inclusion'. *Innovative Higher Education* 43: 303–19.

Settles, I. H., Brassel, S. T., Soranno, P. A. et al. 2019. 'Team Climate Mediates the Effect of Diversity on Environmental Science Team Satisfaction and Data Sharing'. *PloS One* 14: e0219196.

Shamoo, A. and Resnik, D. B. 2015. *Responsible Conduct of Research*, 3rd ed. New York: Oxford University Press.

Shrader-Frechette, K. 2014. *Tainted: How Philosophy of Science Can Expose Bad Science*. New York: Oxford University Press.

Sismondo, S. 2018. *Ghost-Managed Medicine: Big Pharma's Invisible Hands*. Manchester: Mattering Press.

Smith, R. 2005. 'Medical Journals are an Extension of the Marketing Arm of Pharmaceutical Companies'. *PloS Medicine* 2: e138.

Solomon, M. 2001. *Social Empiricism*. Cambridge, MA: MIT Press.

Soranno, P. A., Cheruvelil, K. S., Elliott, K. C. and Montgomery, G. M. 2015. 'It's Good to Share: Why Environmental Scientists' Ethics are Out of Date'. *BioScience* 65: 69–73.

Staley, K. W. 2017. 'Decisions, Decisions: Inductive Risk and the Higgs Boson'. In K. C. Elliott and T. Richards (eds.) *Exploring Inductive Risk: Case Studies of Values in Science*, 37–55. New York: Oxford University Press.

Stanev, R. 2017. 'Inductive Risk and Values in Composite Outcome Measures'. In K. C. Elliott and T. Richards (eds.), *Exploring Inductive Risk: Case Studies of Values in Science*, 171–91. New York: Oxford University Press.

Steel, D. 2010. 'Epistemic Values and the Argument from Inductive Risk'. *Philosophy of Science* 77: 14–34.

Steel, D. 2015. 'Acceptance, Values, and Probability'. *Studies in History and Philosophy of Science* 53: 81–88.

Steel, D. 2017. 'Qualified Epistemic Priority: Comparing Two Approaches to Values in Science'. In K. Elliott and D. Steel (eds.), *Current Controversies in Values and Science*, 49–63. New York: Routledge.

Steel, D. and Whyte, K. 2012. 'Environmental Justice, Values, and Scientific Expertise'. *Kennedy Institute of Ethics Journal* 22: 163–82.

Steele, K. 2012. 'The Scientist Qua Policy Advisor Makes Value Judgements'. *Philosophy of Science* 79: 893–904.

Stegenga, J. 2017. 'Drug Regulation and the Inductive Risk Calculus'. In K. Elliott and T. Richards (eds.), *Exploring Inductive Risk: Case Studies of Values in Science*, 17–36. New York: Oxford University Press.

Stegenga, J. 2018. *Medical Nihilism*. Oxford: Oxford University Press.

Valles, S. A. 2018. *Philosophy of Population Health: Philosophy for a New Public Health Era*. New York: Routledge.

Valles, S. A. 2020. 'The Predictable Inequities of COVID-19 in the US: Fundamental Causes and Broken Institutions'. *Kennedy Institute of Ethics Journal* 30: 191–214.

Viala-Gaudefroy, G. and Lindaman, D. 2020. 'Donald Trump's "Chinese Virus": The Politics of Naming'. *The Conversation* (21 April). https://thecon versation.com/donald-trumps-chinese-virus-the-politics-of-naming-136796

Ward, Z. 2021. 'On Value-Laden Science'. *Studies in History and Philosophy of Science* 85: 54–62.

Weingart, P. and Padberg, B., eds. 2014. *University Experiments in Interdisciplinarity: Obstacles and Opportunities*. Bielefeld: transcript Verlag.

Whyte, K. P., Dockry, M., Baule, W. and Fellman, D. 2014. 'Supporting Tribal Climate Change Adaptation Planning through Community Participatory Strategic Foresight Scenario Development'. In: *Project Reports*. D. Brown, W. Baule, L. E. Briley and E. Gibbons, eds. Available from the Great Lakes Integrated Sciences and Assessments (GLISA) Center. http://glisa.umich.edu /media/files/projectreports/GLISA_ProjRep_Strategic-Foresight.pdf

Wickson, F. and Wynne, B. 2012. 'Ethics of Science for Policy in the Environmental Governance of Biotechnology: MON810 Maize in Europe'. *Ethics, Policy & Environment* 15: 321–40.

Wilholt, T. 2009. 'Bias and Values in Scientific Research'. *Studies in History and Philosophy of Science* 40: 92–101.

Winsberg, E. 2018. *Philosophy and Climate Science*. Cambridge: Cambridge University Press.

Zihlman, A. 1985. 'Gathering Stories for Hunting Human Nature'. *Feminist Studies* 11: 365–77.

Acknowledgements

I am very grateful to Jacob Stegenga for inviting me to write this Element and for giving me helpful feedback on the manuscript. I had the good fortune of being on sabbatical during most of the writing process, so I owe thanks to Michigan State University and my primary academic units, Lyman Briggs College and the Department of Fisheries and Wildlife, for granting me the sabbatical leave to work on this and other projects. I was also very fortunate to receive input from six people who read through the entire manuscript and provided excellent feedback: Robyn Bluhm, Stephanie Harvard, Kristen Intemann, Soazig LeBihan, Dan McKaughan, and Drew Schroeder. In addition, I received wonderful advice from the undergraduate students in a seminar taught by Drew Schroeder at Claremont McKenna College during the spring semester of 2022. The final manuscript is significantly improved thanks to all the insights I received from these generous readers, as well as the guidance of Inmaculada de Melo-Martín and another reviewer for Cambridge University Press. The remaining weaknesses are of course my own fault and not theirs!

My work is also deeply influenced by those with whom I have collaborated. I am especially indebted to David Resnik, whose work with me played an important role in the fifth section of this Element. My collaborations with Dan McKaughan have also played a major role in my thinking about values in science. In addition, I am grateful to Erin Cech, Kendra Cheruvelil, Georgina Montgomery, and Isis Settles, who have taught me a great deal about the climate on science teams and its role in promoting the ethical values of diversity, equity, and inclusion. My thinking about the nature of engaged philosophy of science has been greatly enriched by working with Katie Plaisance. Finally, my scholarship has been strengthened through countless conversations with a wide array of wonderful colleagues at workshops and conferences. In addition to those I have already mentioned, I think especially of Justin Biddle, Matthew Brown, Heather Douglas, Joyce Havstad, Dan Hicks, Bennett Holman, Stephen John, Rebecca Korf, Janet Kourany, Hugh Lacey, Kristina Rolin, Phyllis Rooney, Dan Steel, Sean Valles, Zina Ward, and Torsten Wilholt, but I am sure that I am forgetting many others who have helped me sharpen the ideas that appear in this Element.

Finally, my deepest thanks go to my family. I will always be grateful to my parents, Cris and Janelle, for their encouragement and support. Meanwhile, it has been thrilling to watch my children, Jayden and Leah, mature throughout the years I have been thinking and writing about values in science. It is now delightful to be able to talk about my philosophical ideas with them (although the delight might be more on my part than on theirs). And, of course, I am most grateful to my partner, Janet. She is unfailingly encouraging, understanding, and patient. All of my scholarship is deeply informed by her love and support.

Philosophy of Science

Jacob Stegenga

University of Cambridge

Jacob Stegenga is a Reader in the Department of History and Philosophy of Science at the University of Cambridge. He has published widely on fundamental topics in reasoning and rationality and philosophical problems in medicine and biology. Prior to joining Cambridge he taught in the United States and Canada, and he received his PhD from the University of California San Diego.

About the Series

This series of Elements in Philosophy of Science provides an extensive overview of the themes, topics and debates which constitute the philosophy of science. Distinguished specialists provide an up-to-date summary of the results of current research on their topics, as well as offering their own take on those topics and drawing original conclusions.

Cambridge Elements ⁼

Philosophy of Science

Printed in the United States
by Baker & Taylor Publisher Services